THE CRACKS IN EVERYTHING

BRANT SLOMOVIC

KEHRƎR

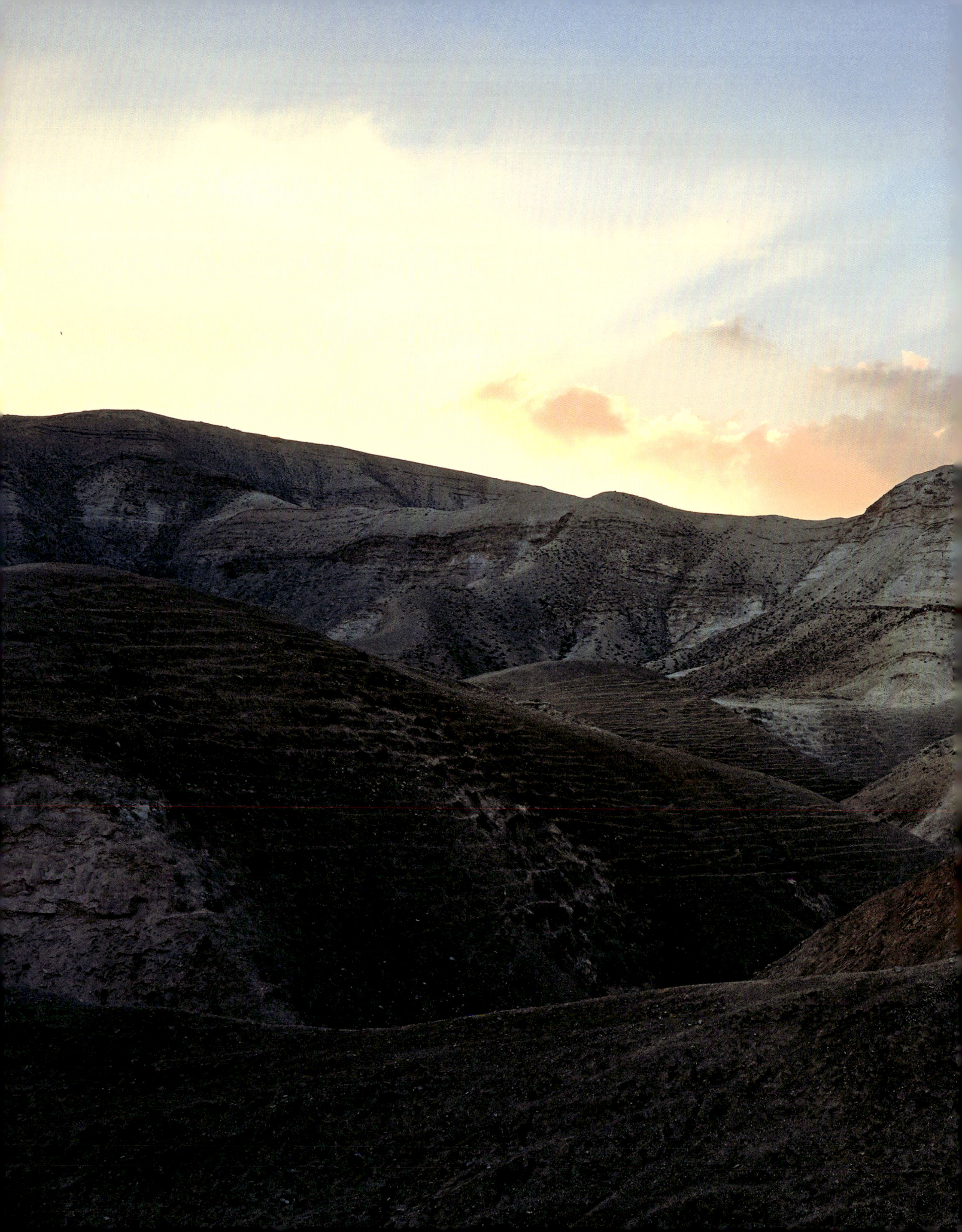

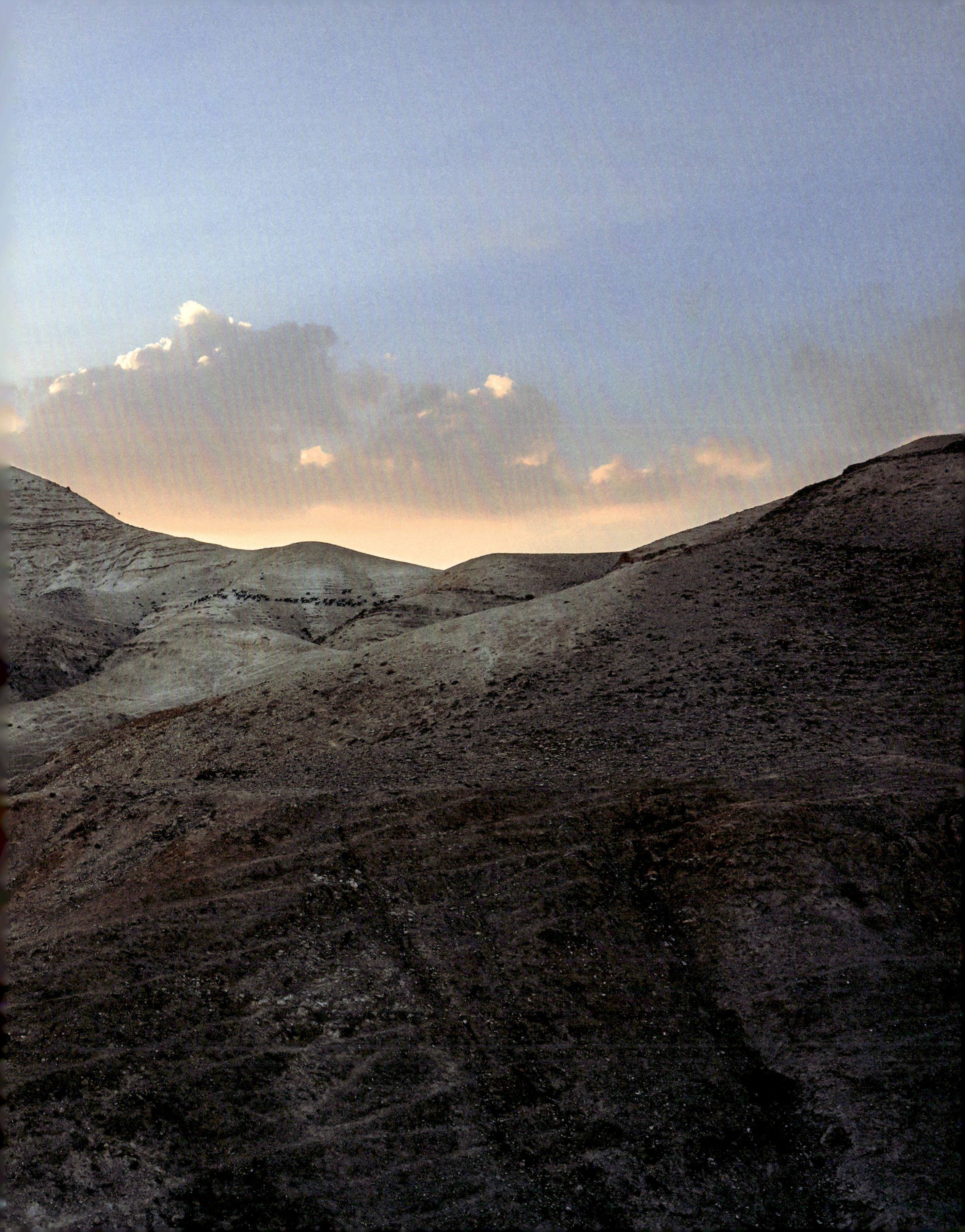

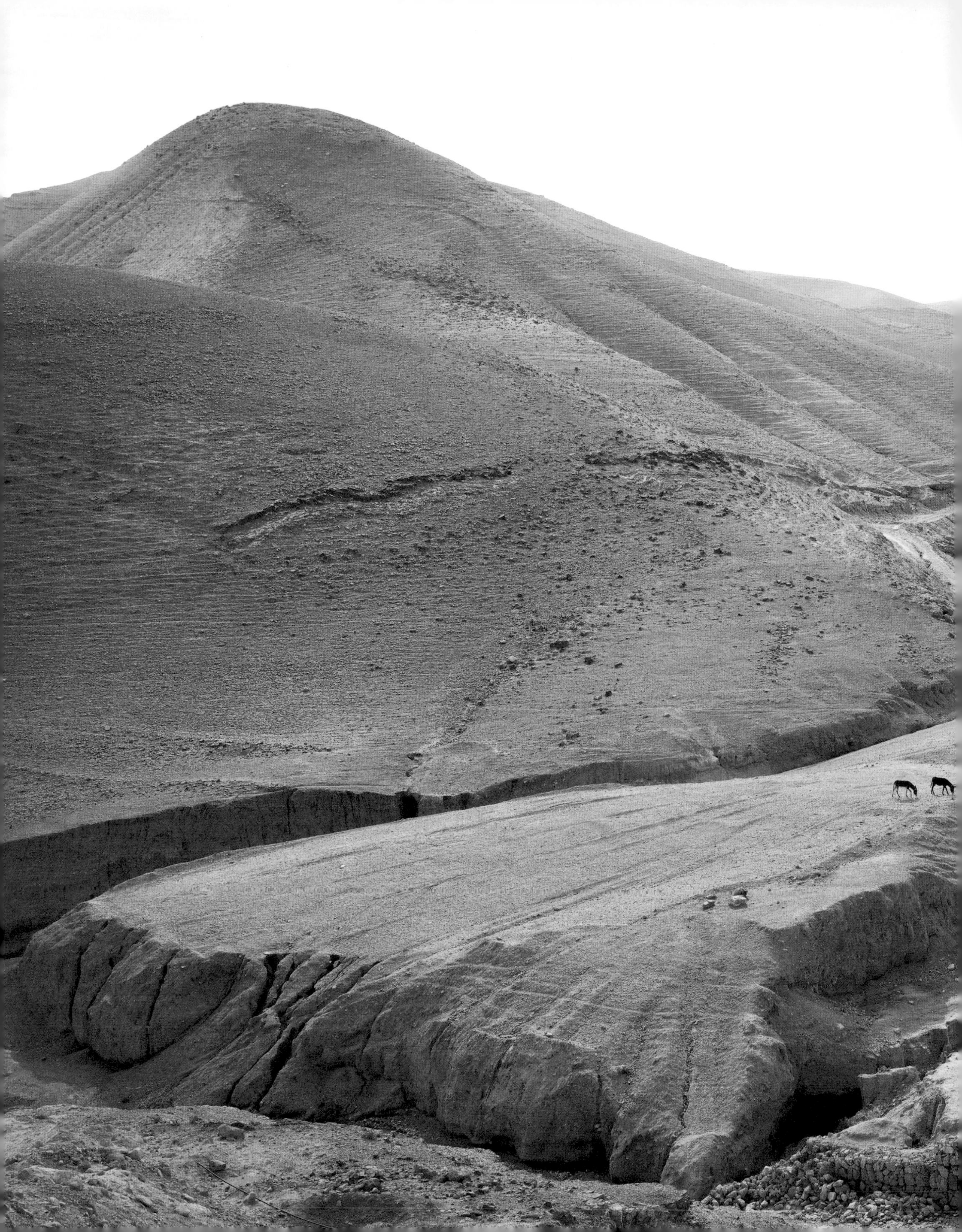

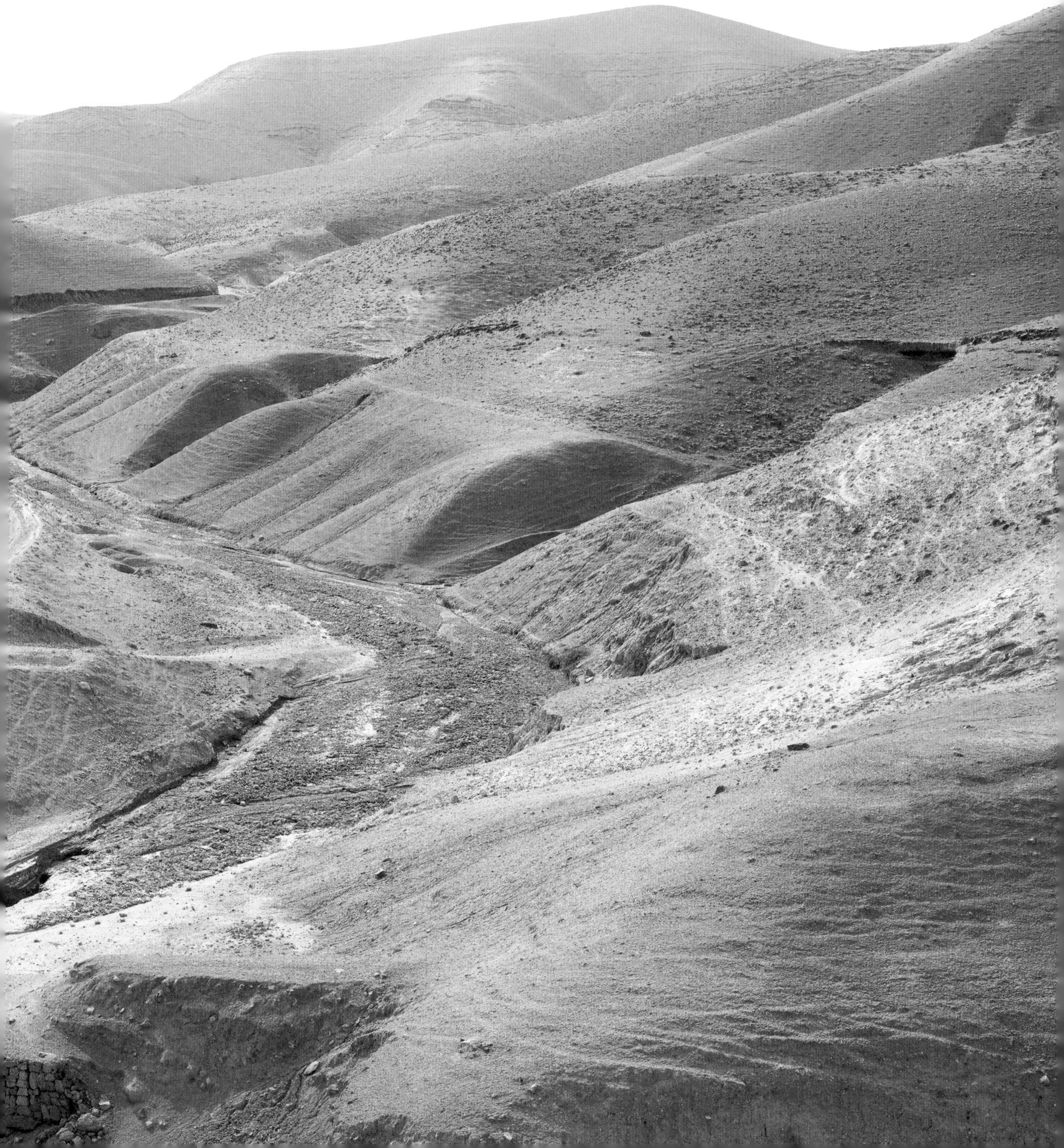

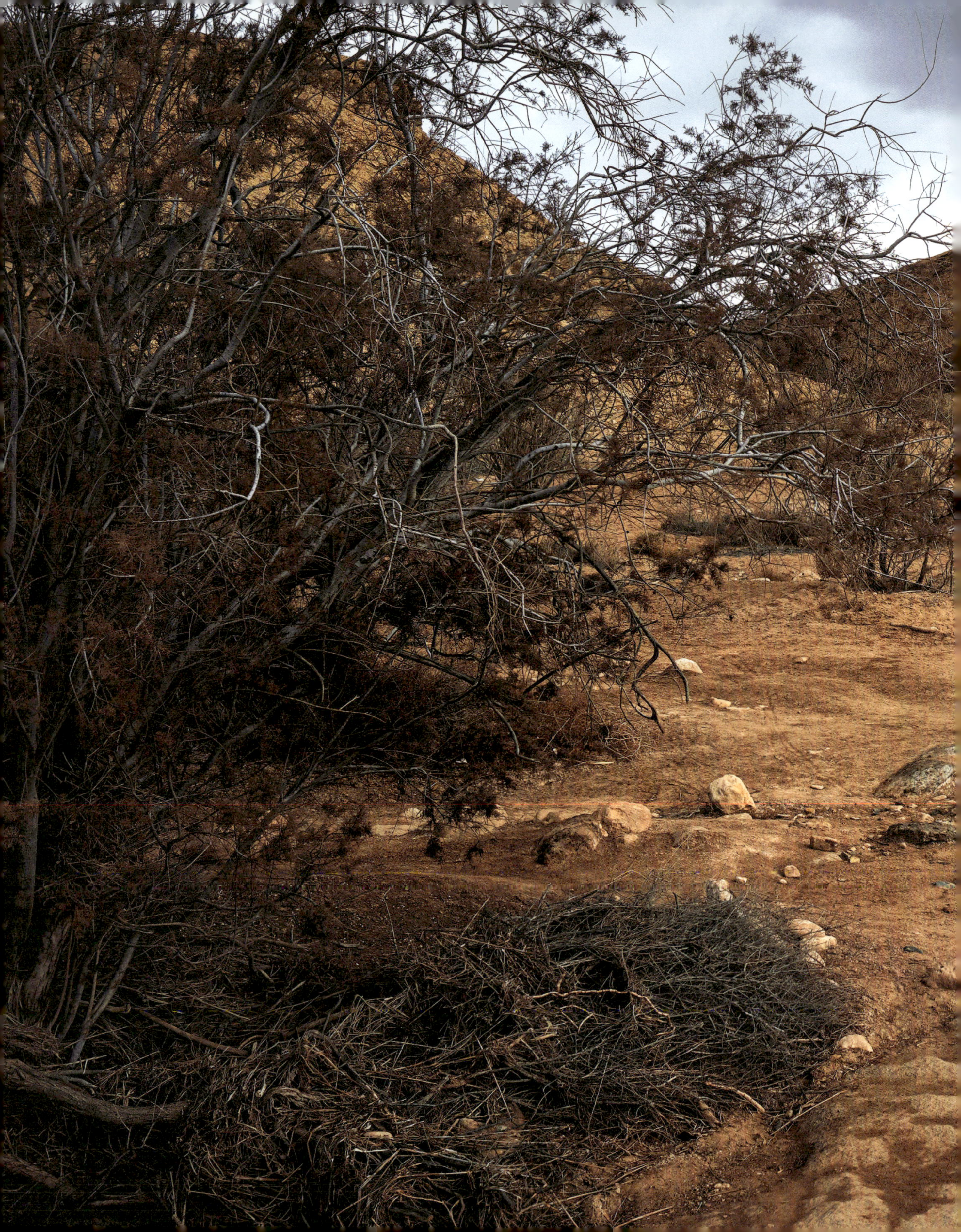

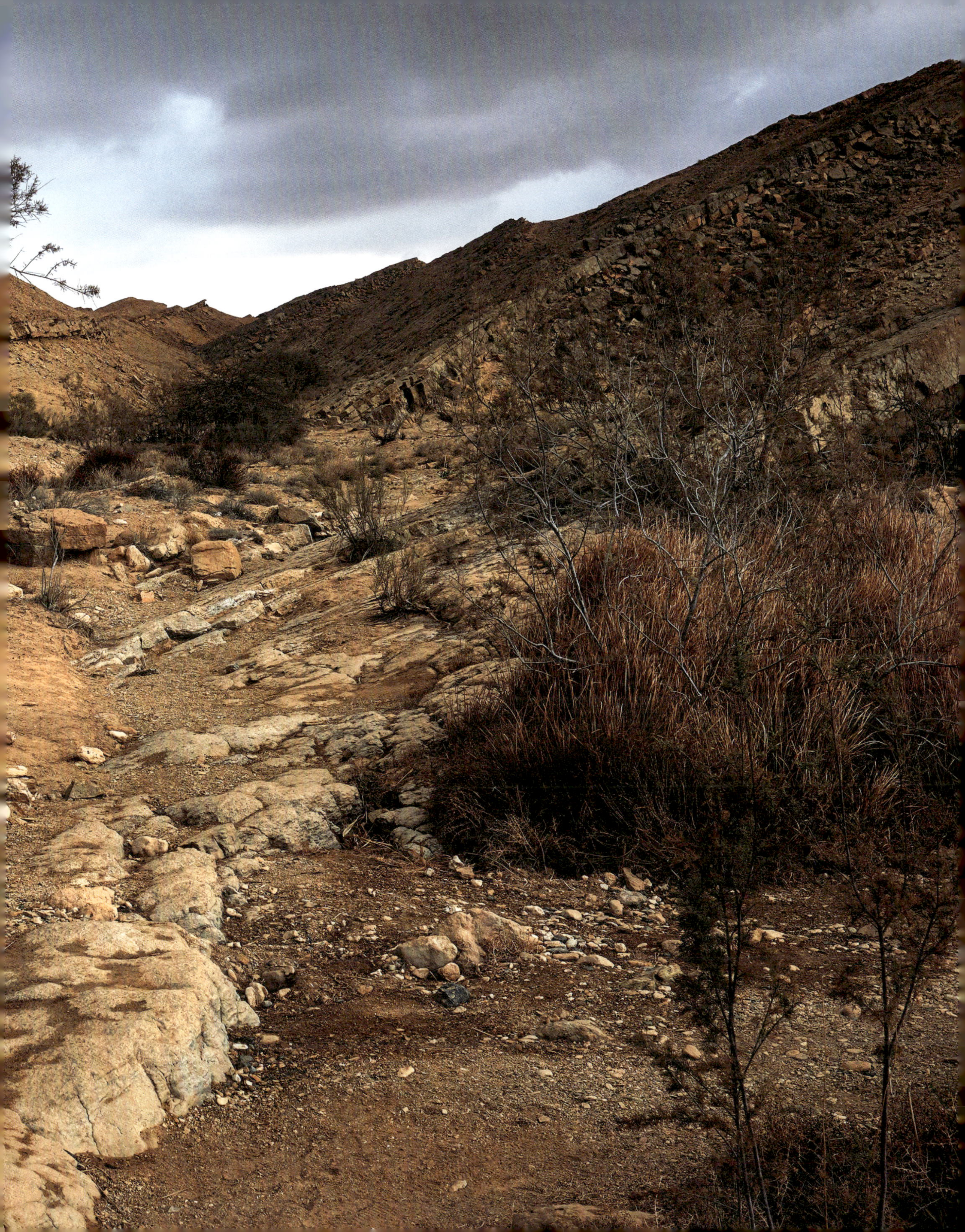

"Humans don't mind hardship, in fact they thrive on it;
what they mind is not feeling necessary..."

Sebastian Junger

Leah | 19 | Los Angeles, California, USA | Infantry

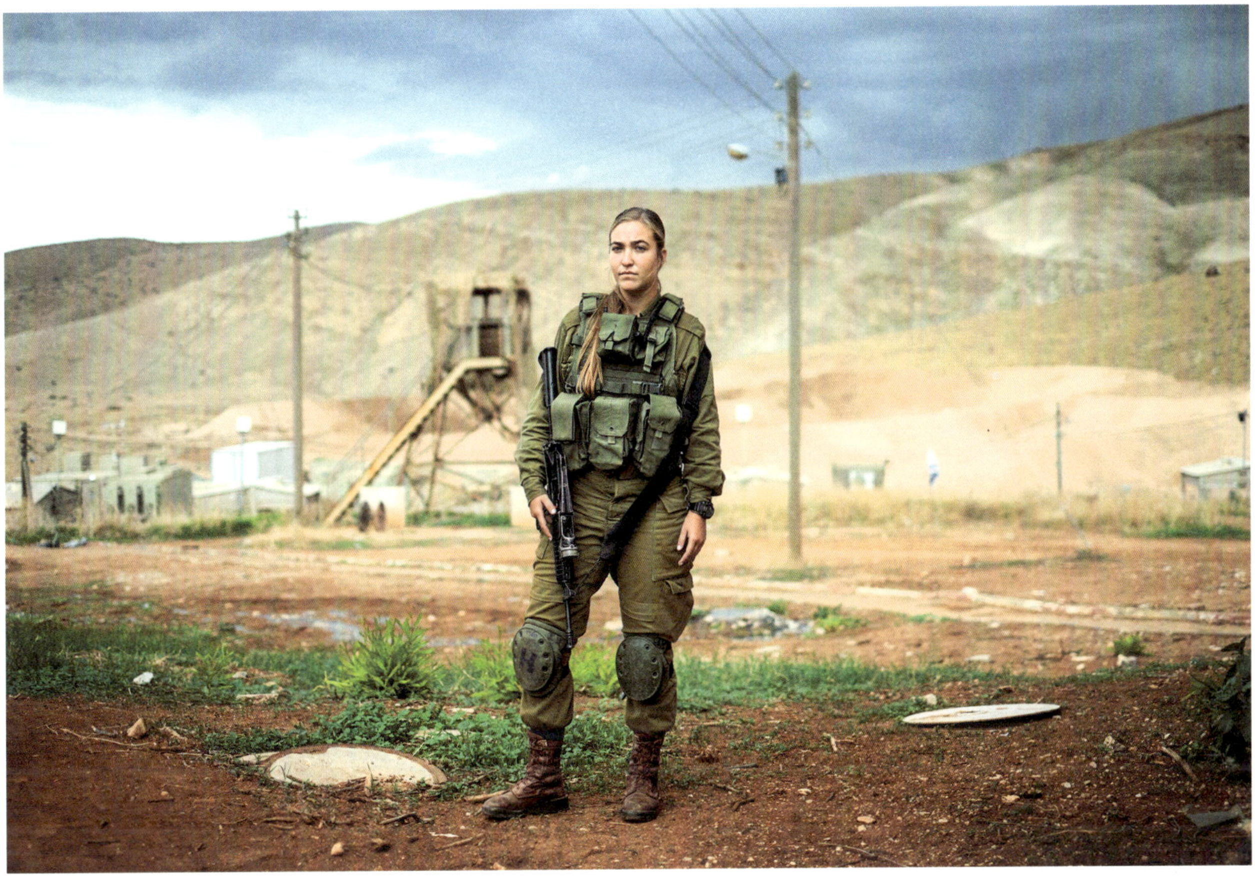

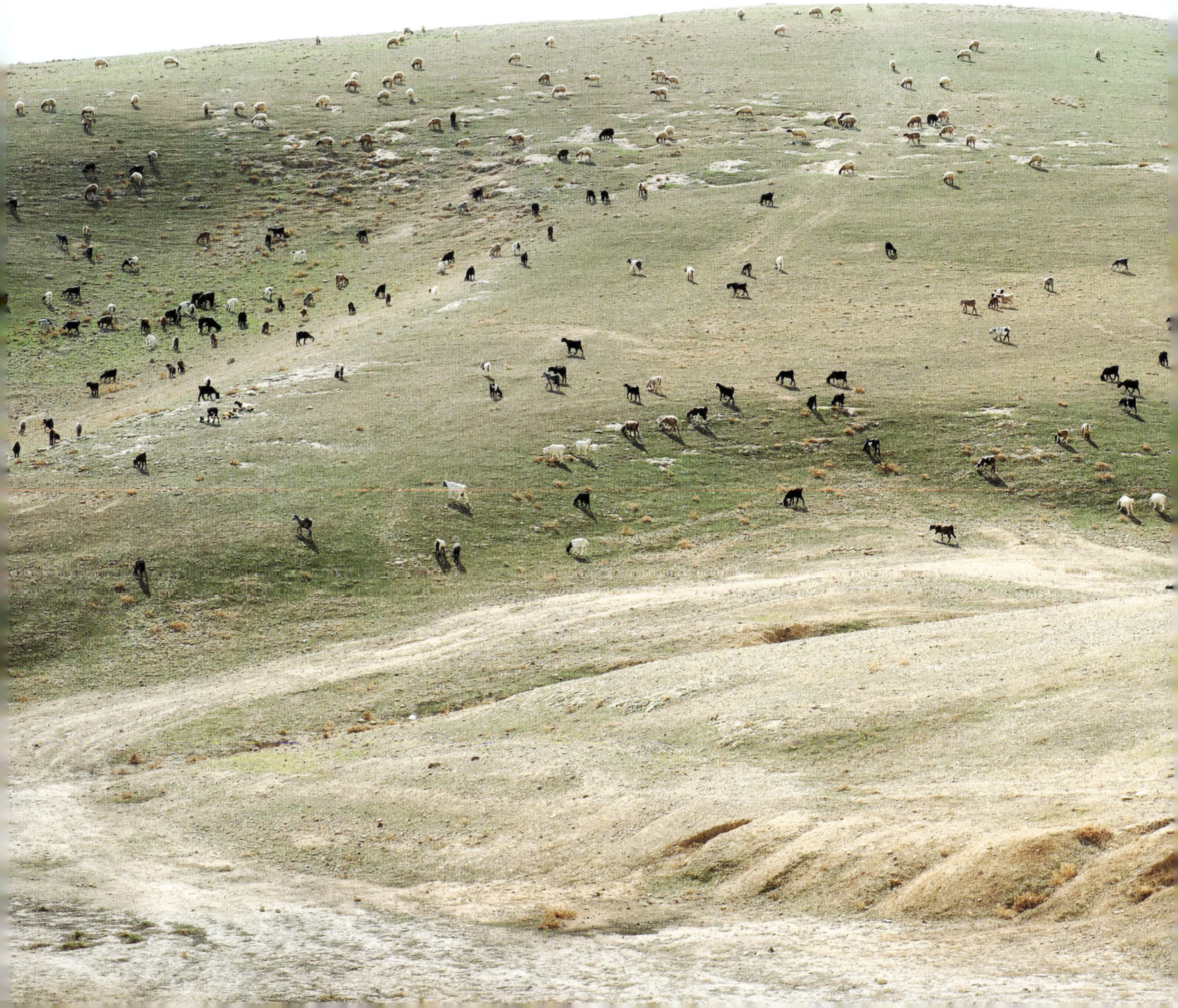

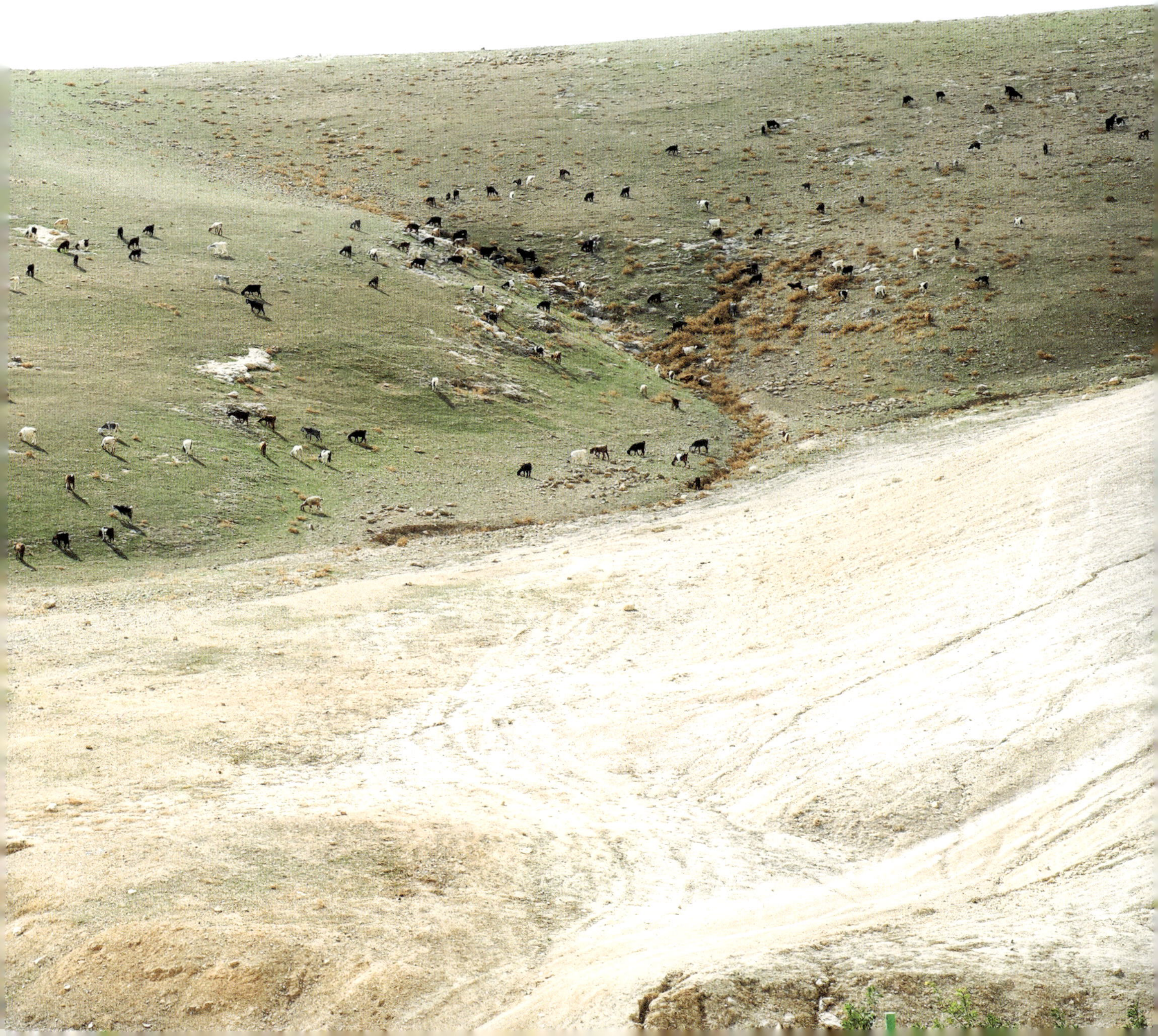

Sisit | 21 | Addis Ababa, Ethiopia | Infantry

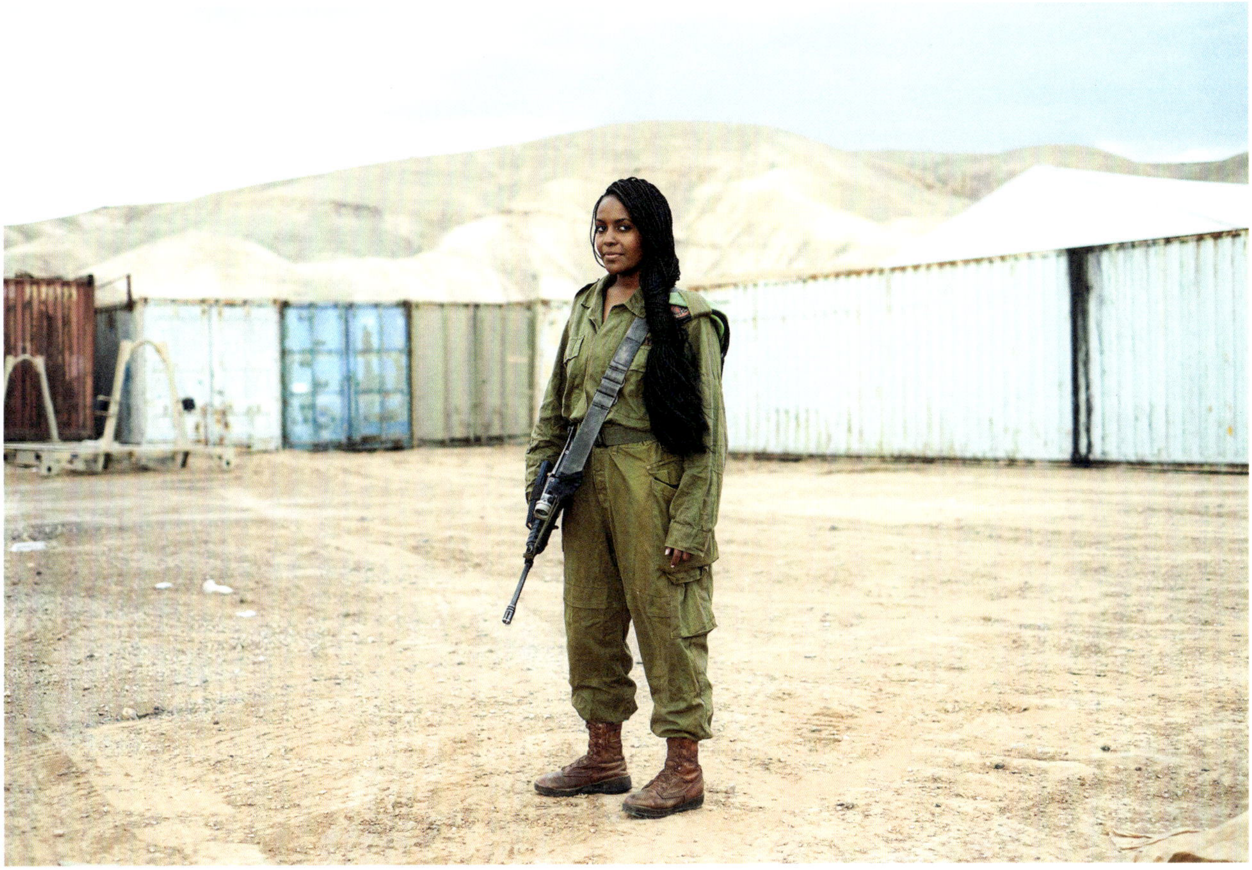

Chai | 19 | Ko Pha Ngan, Thailand | Infantry

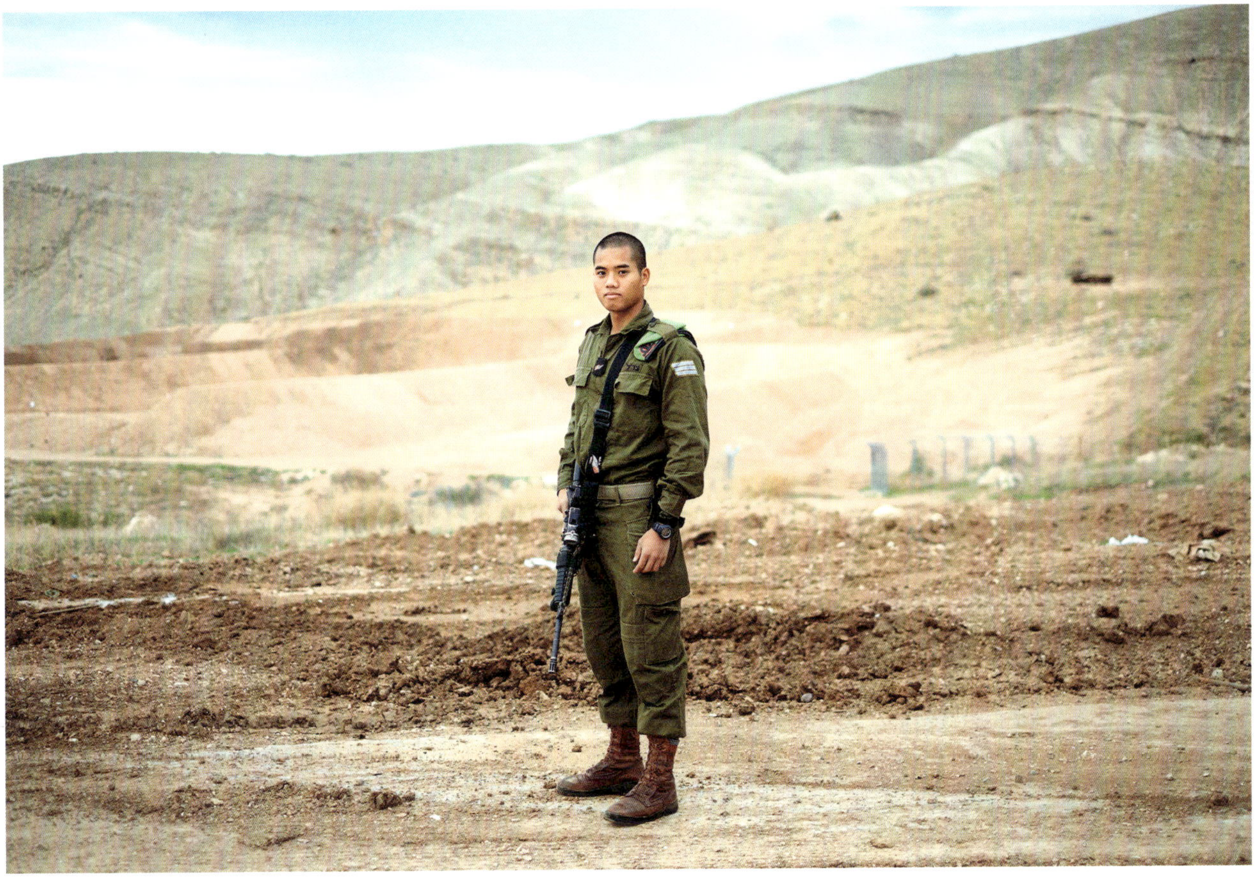

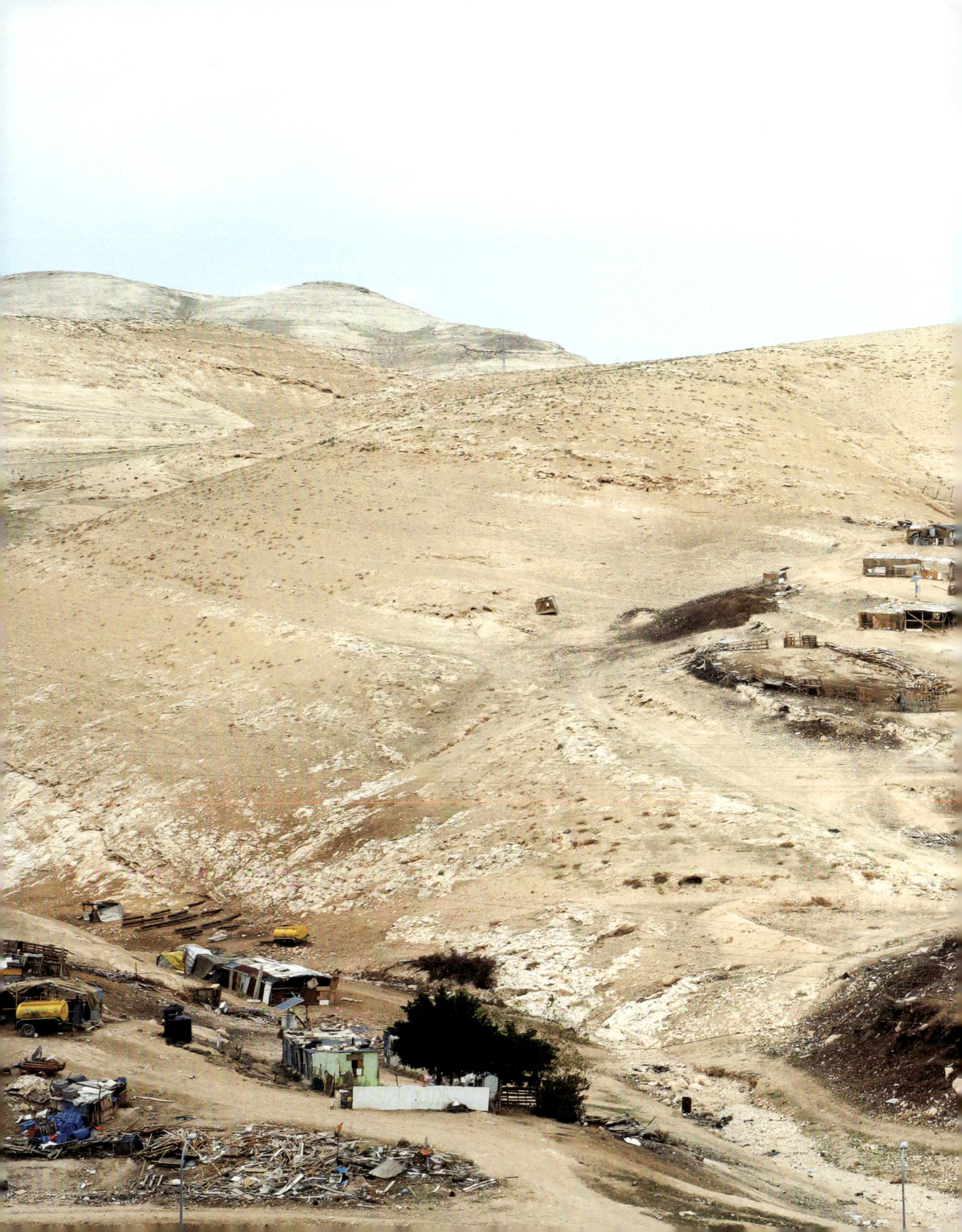

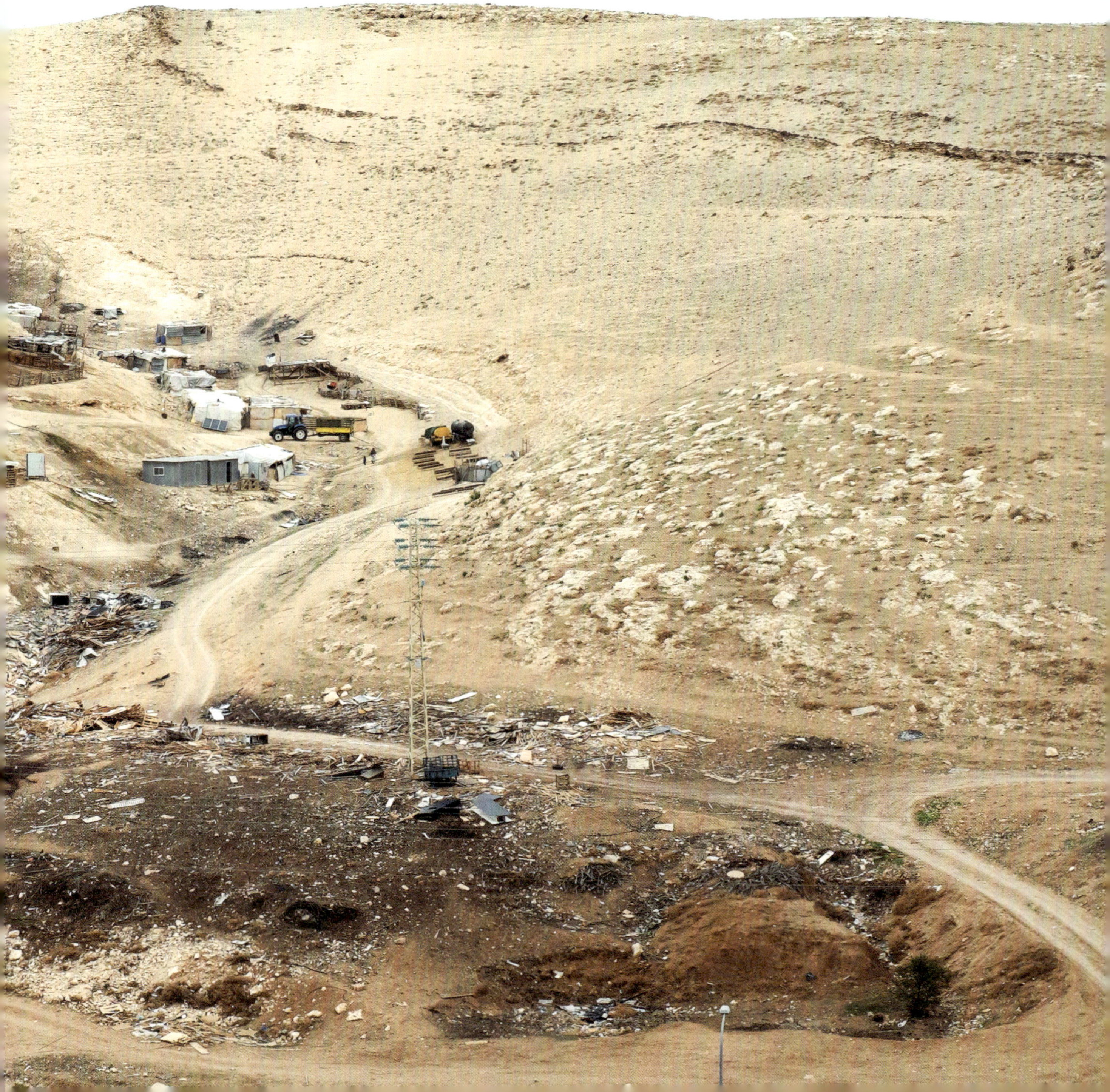

Emily | 19 | Undisclosed, Uzbekistan | Infantry

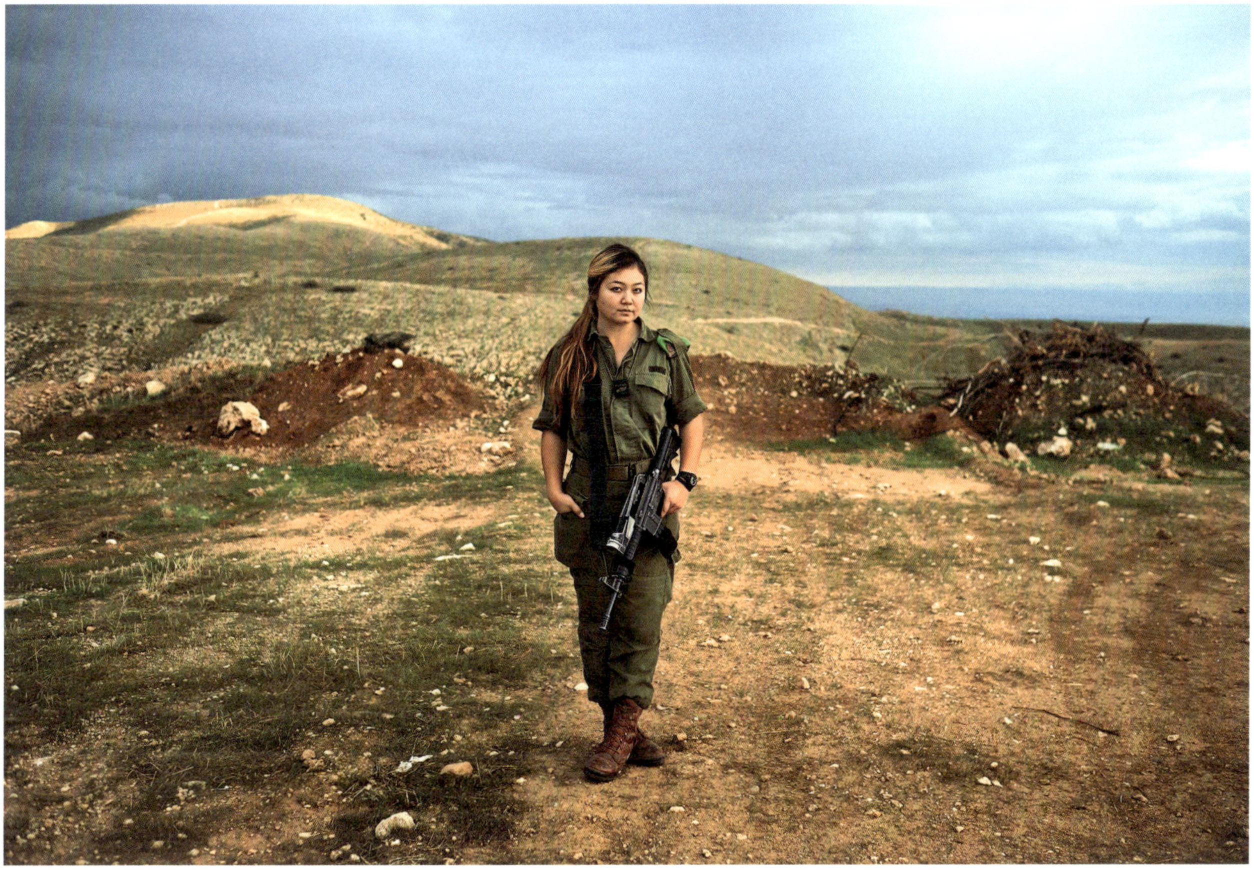

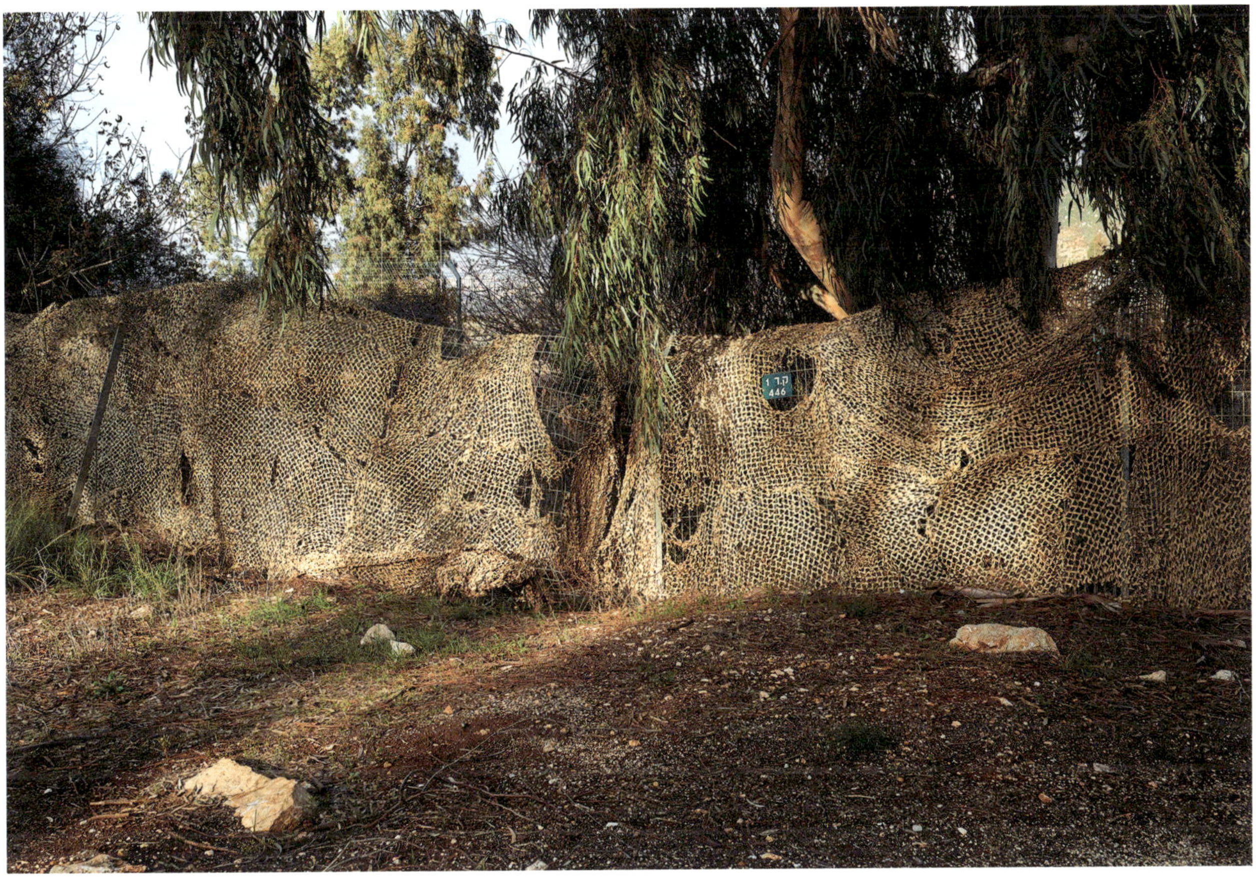
ק.ד 1
446

"Stas" | 19 | Gomel, Belarus | Logistics

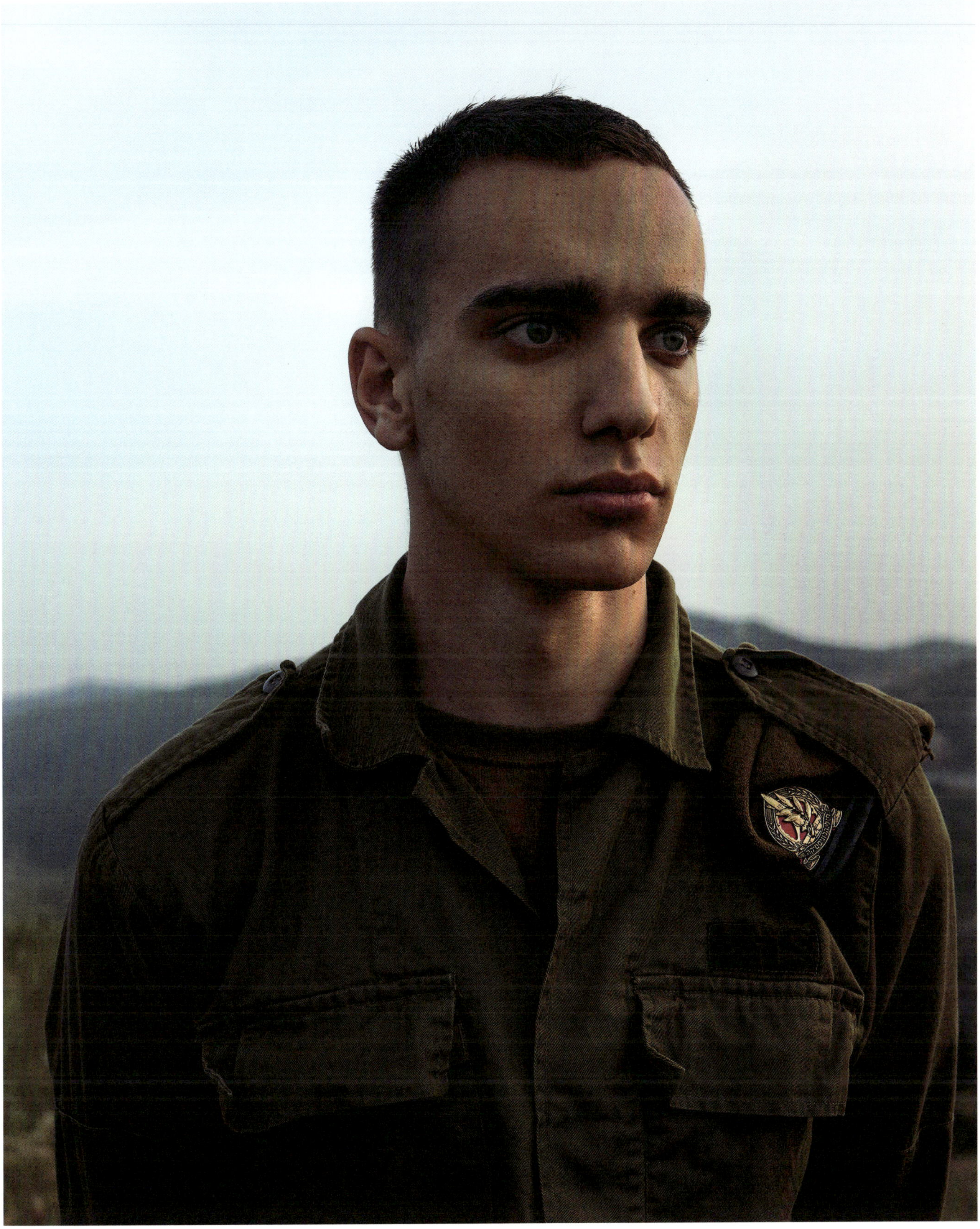

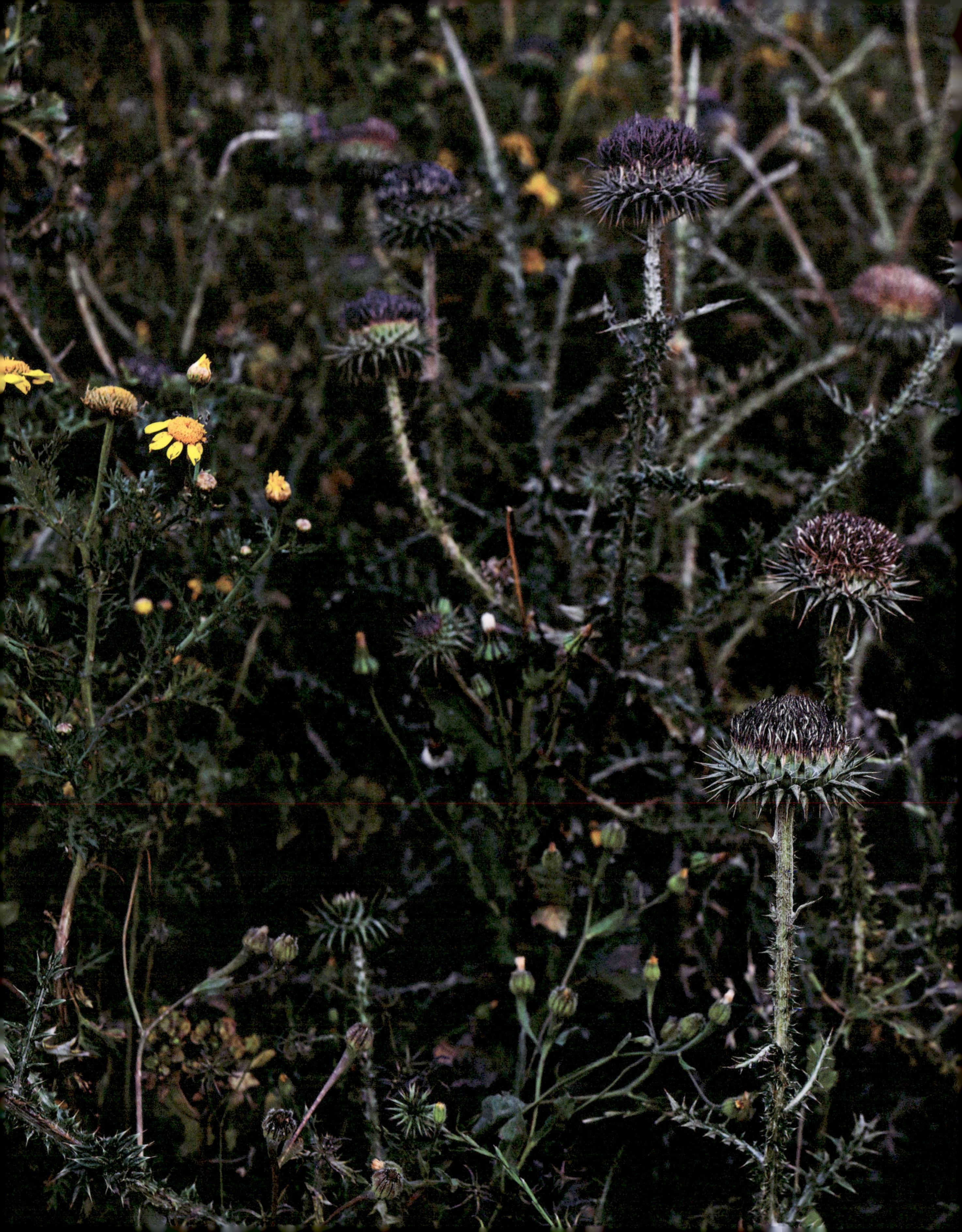

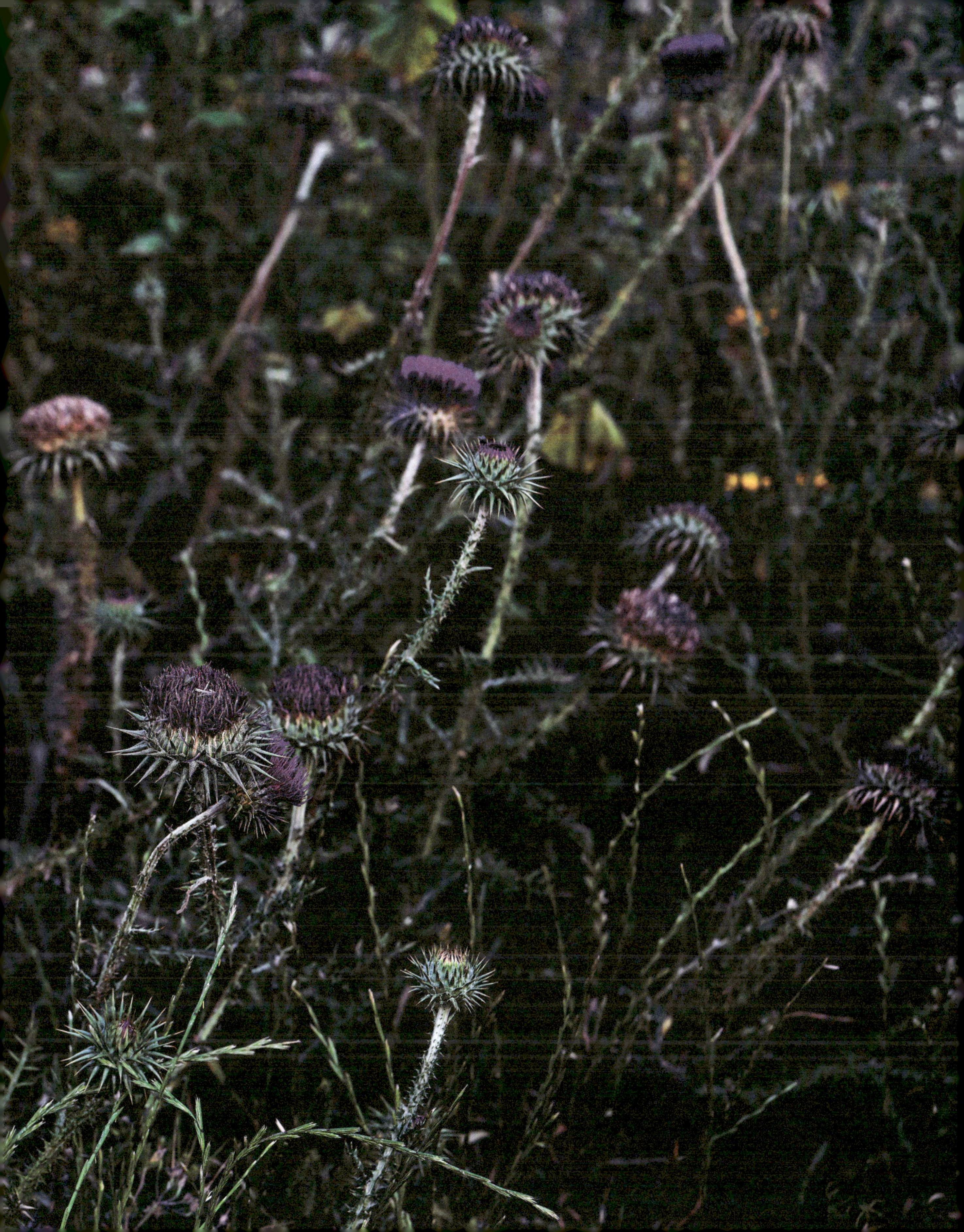

Harrison | 23 | New York, New York, USA | Infantry

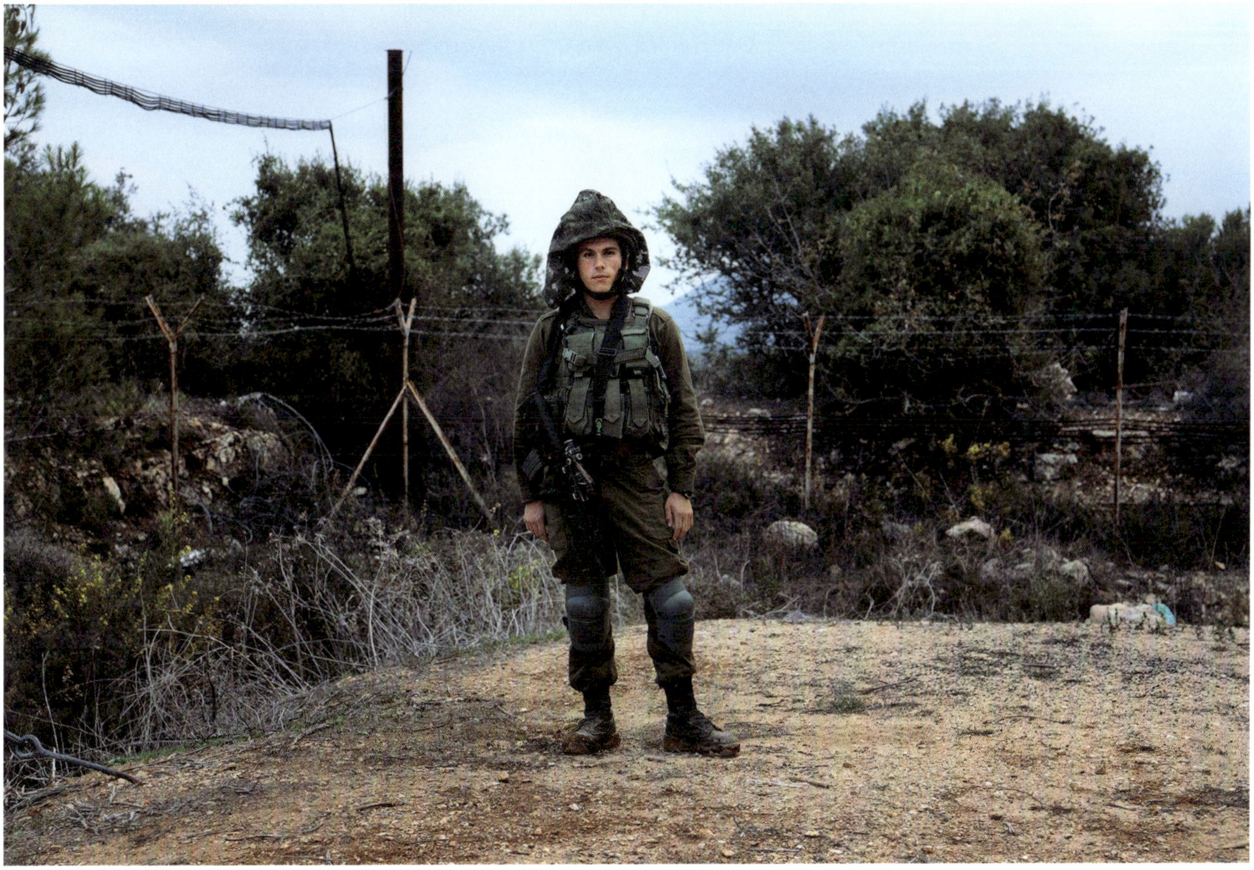

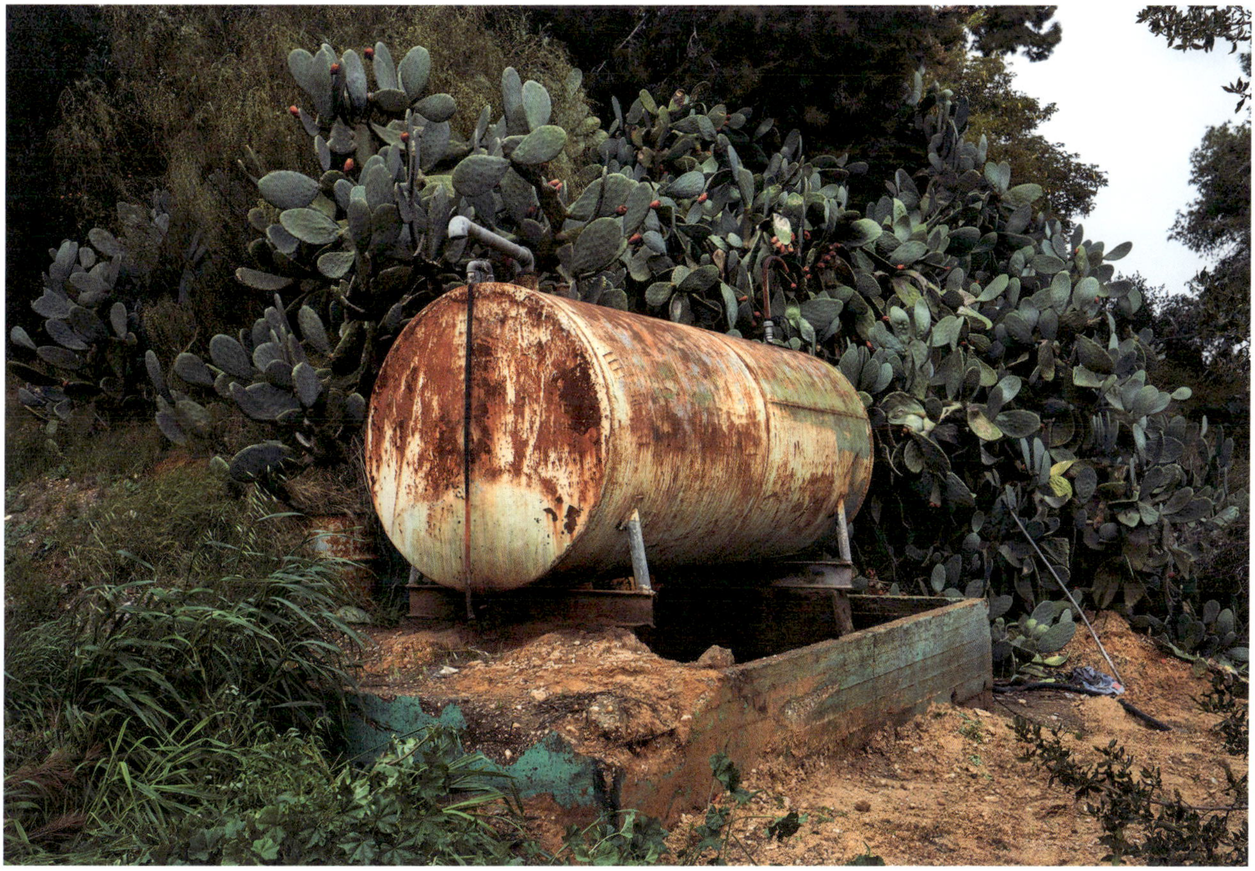

Sara | 21 | Five Towns, New York, USA | Artillery

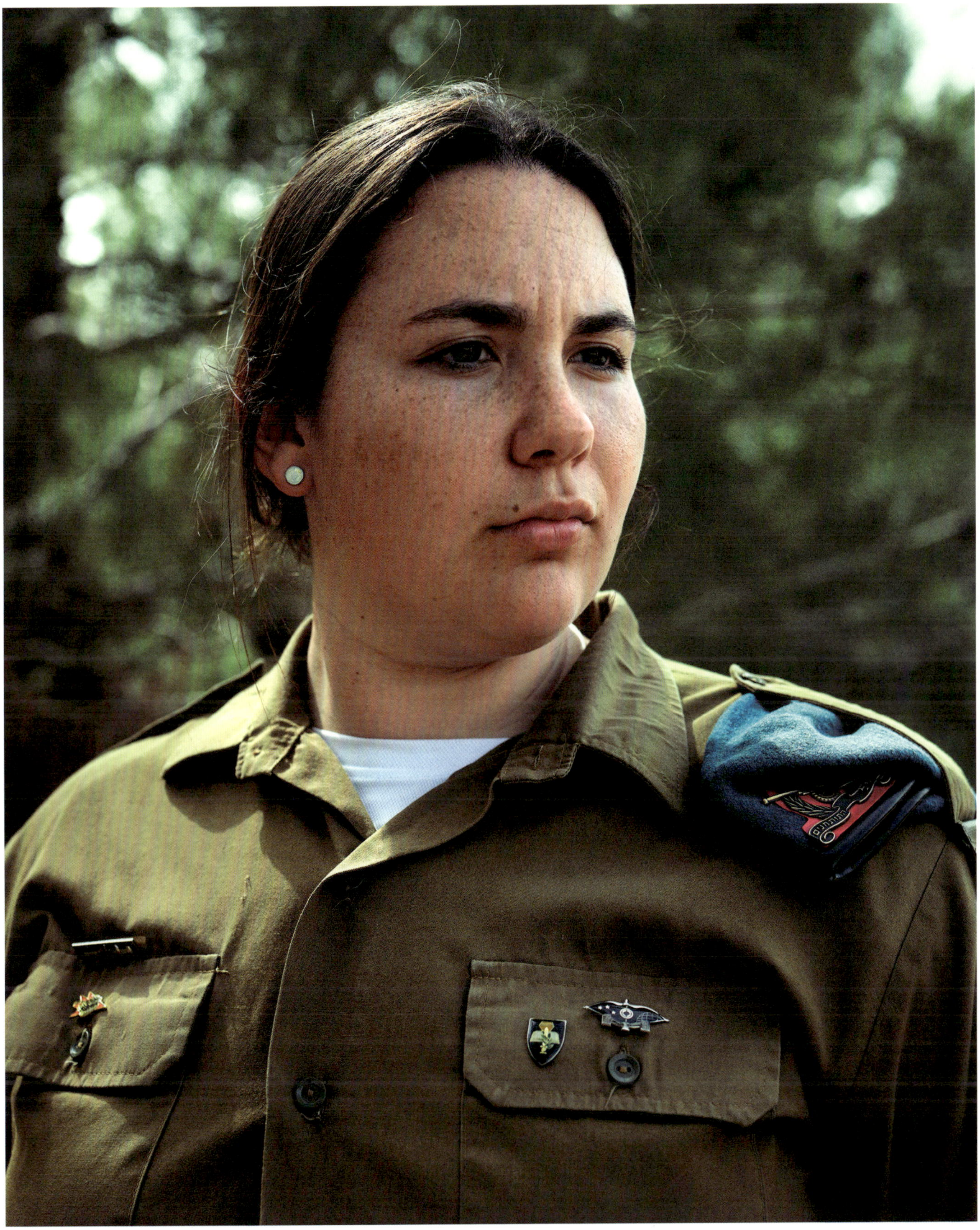

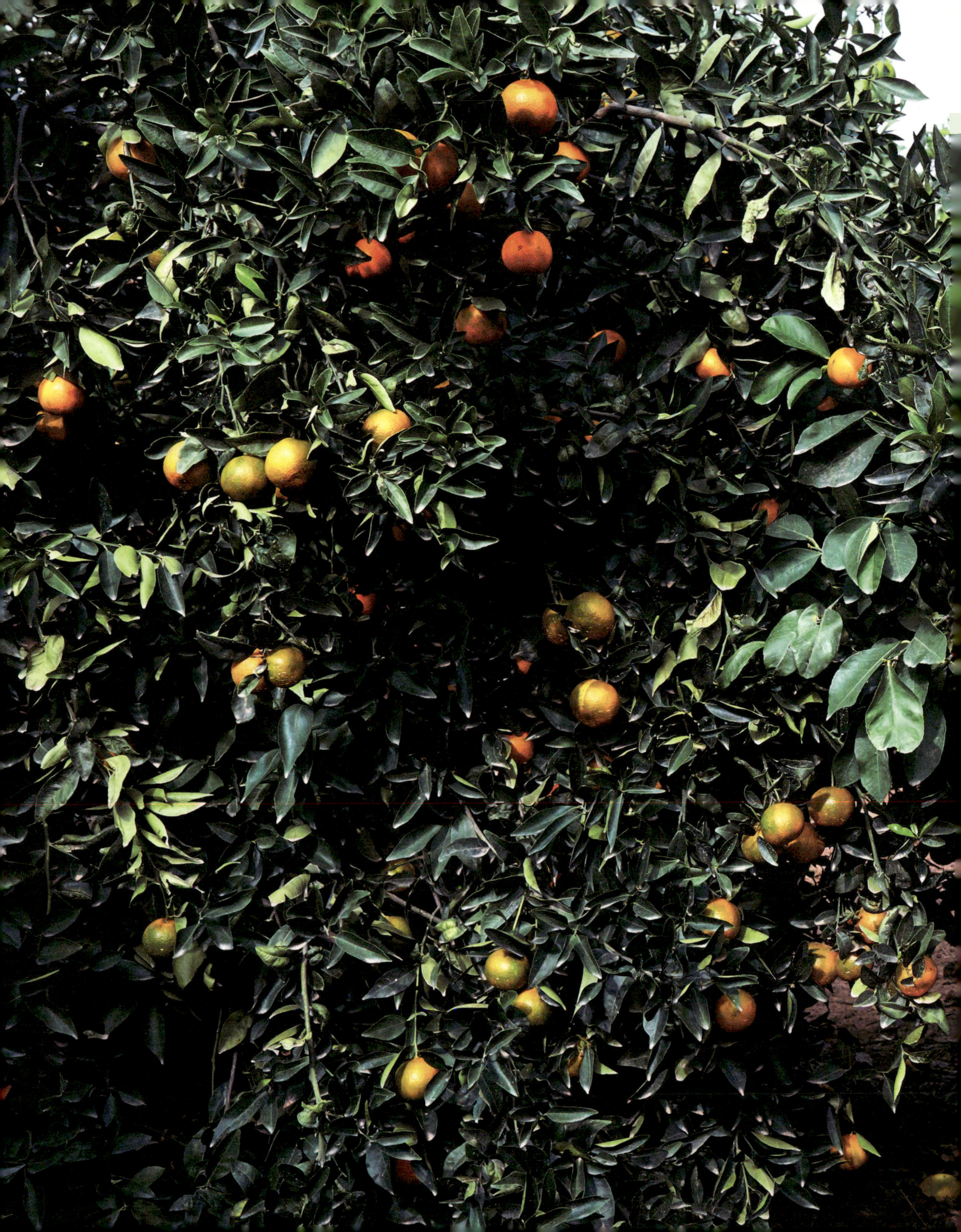

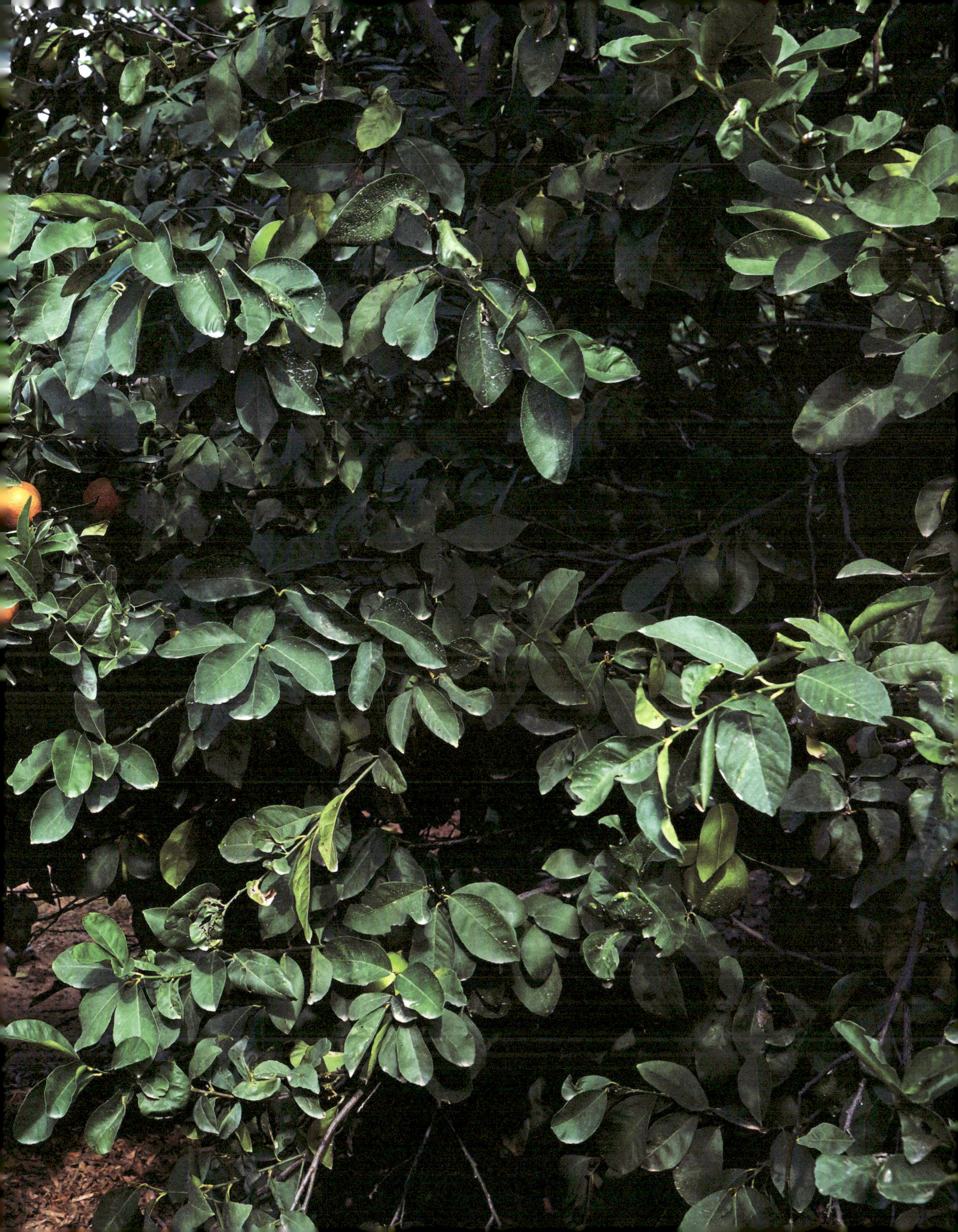

Peter | 18 | Minsk, Belarus | Urban Search and Rescue

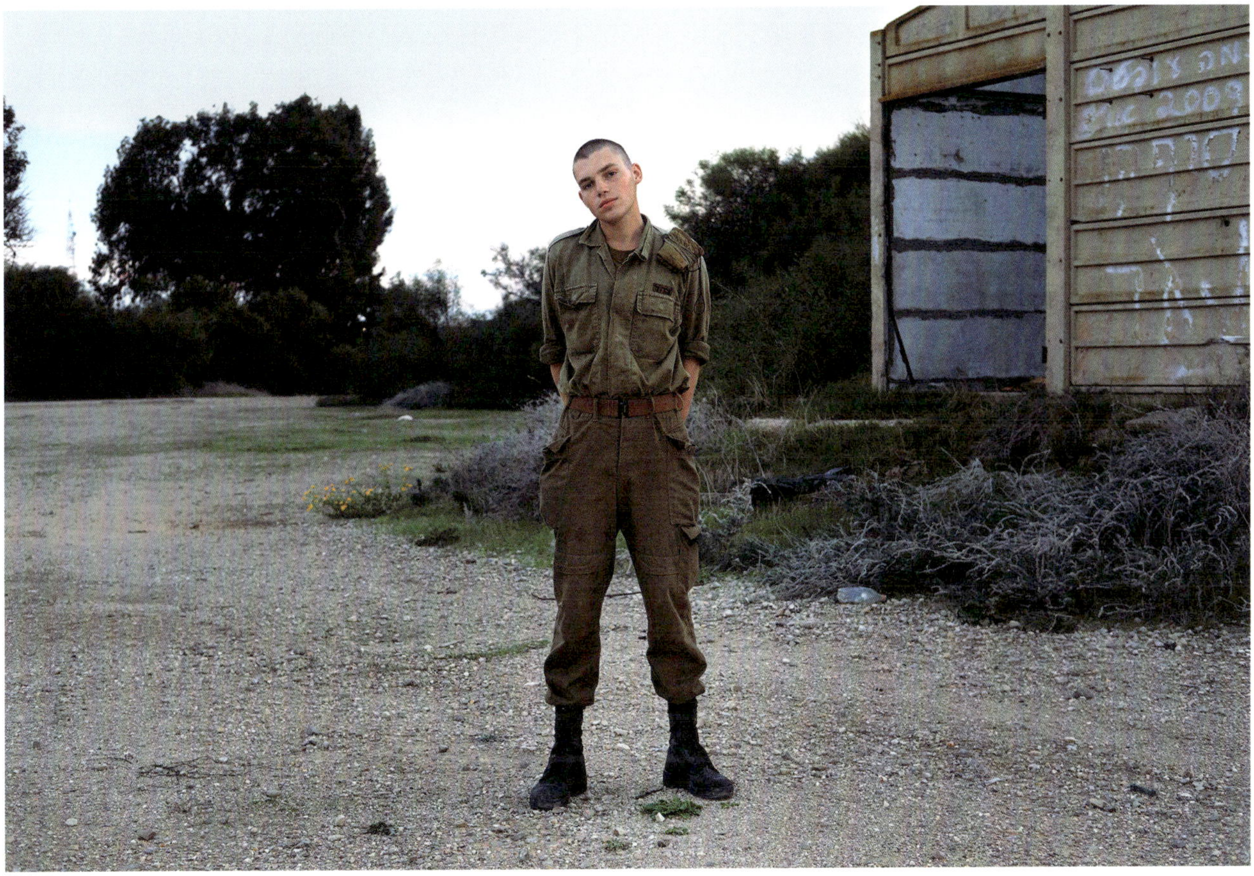

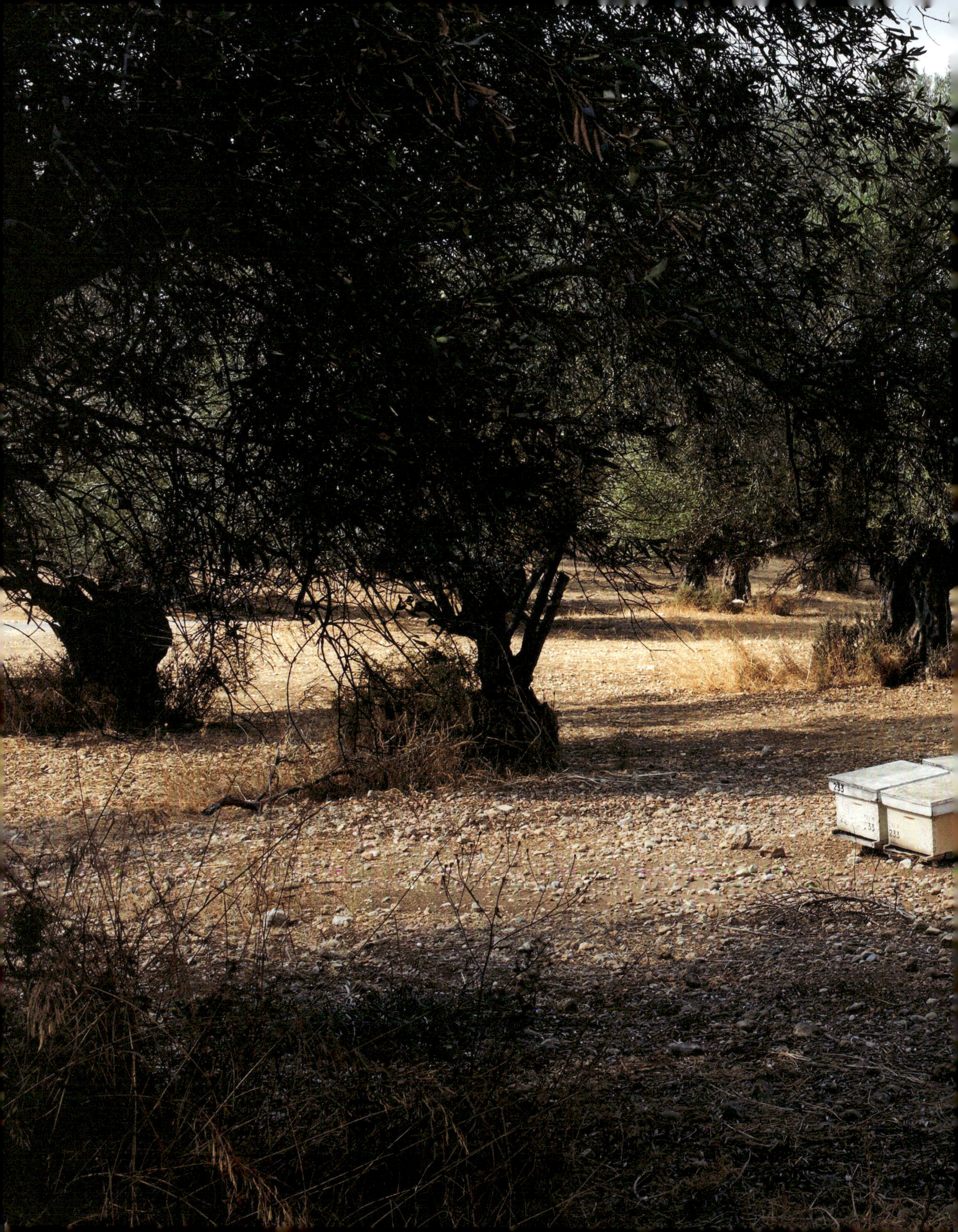

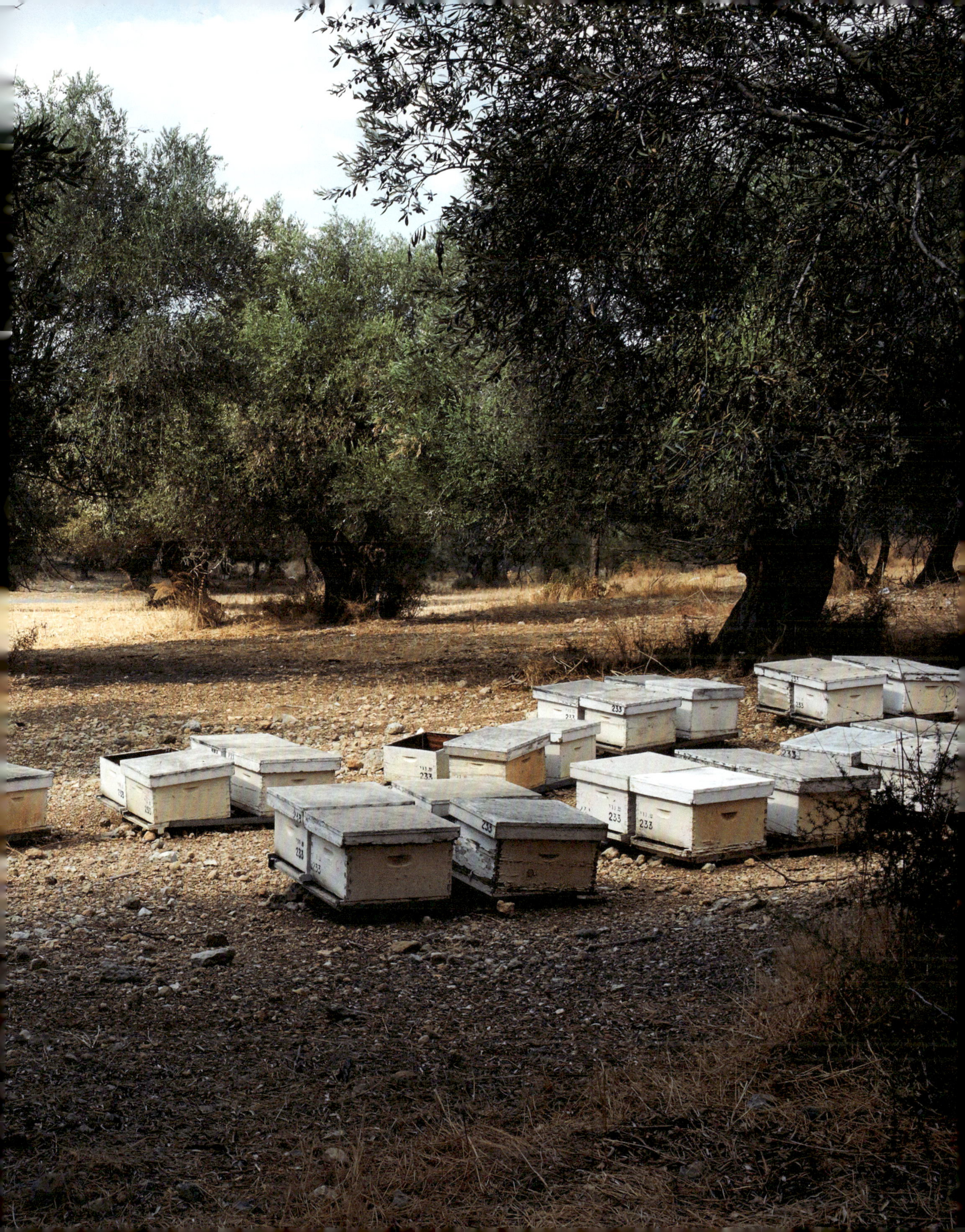
233

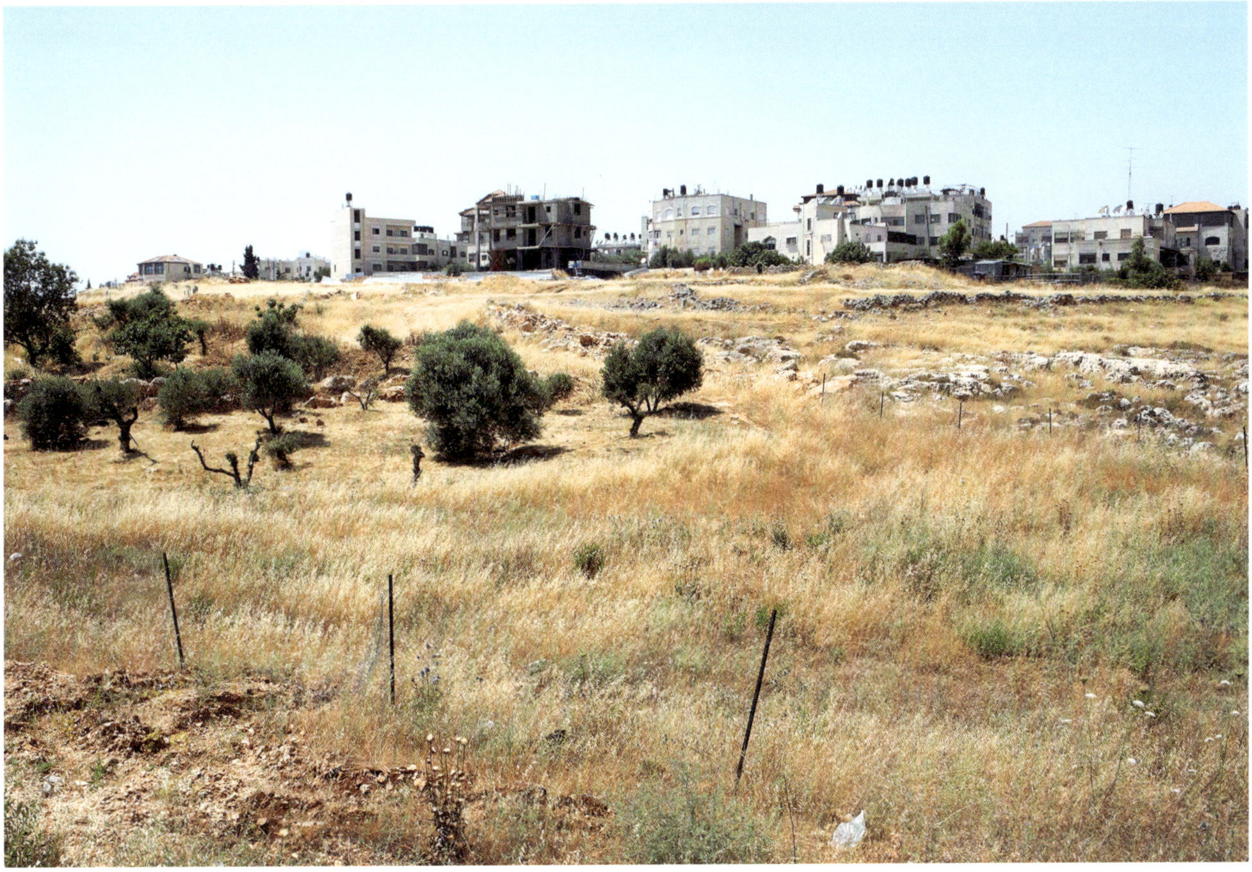

Denis | 20 | Undisclosed, Kazakhstan | Military Police Corps

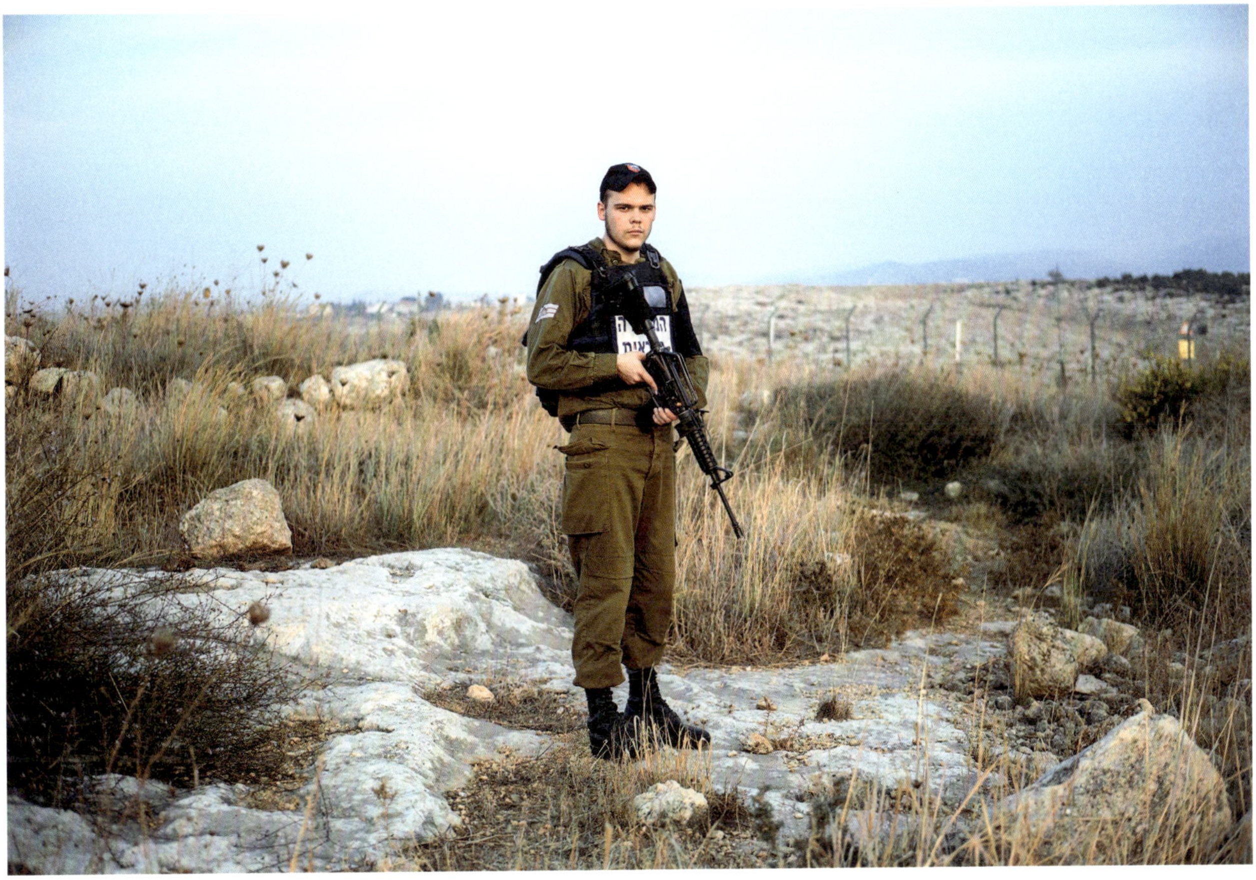

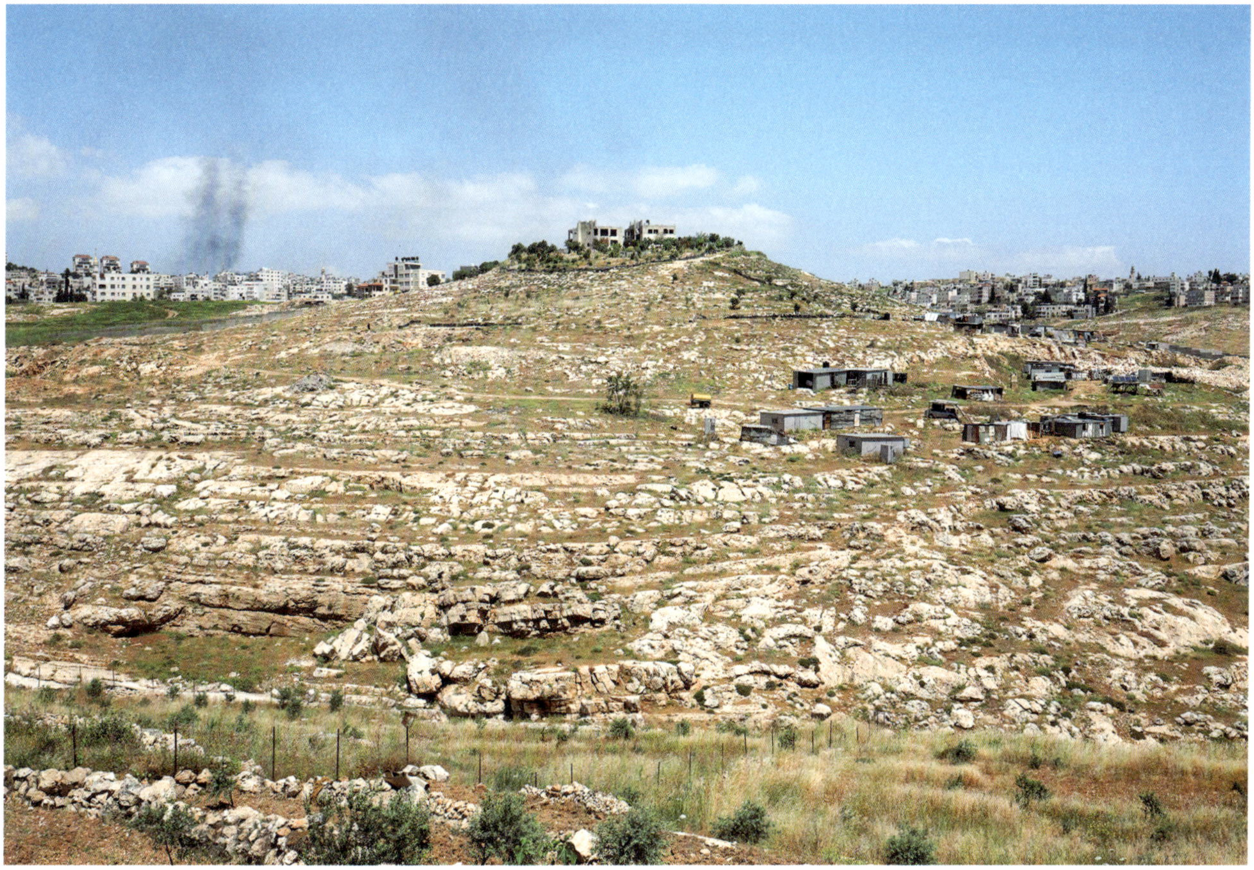

Sergey | 19 | Saint Petersburg, Russia | Military Police Corps

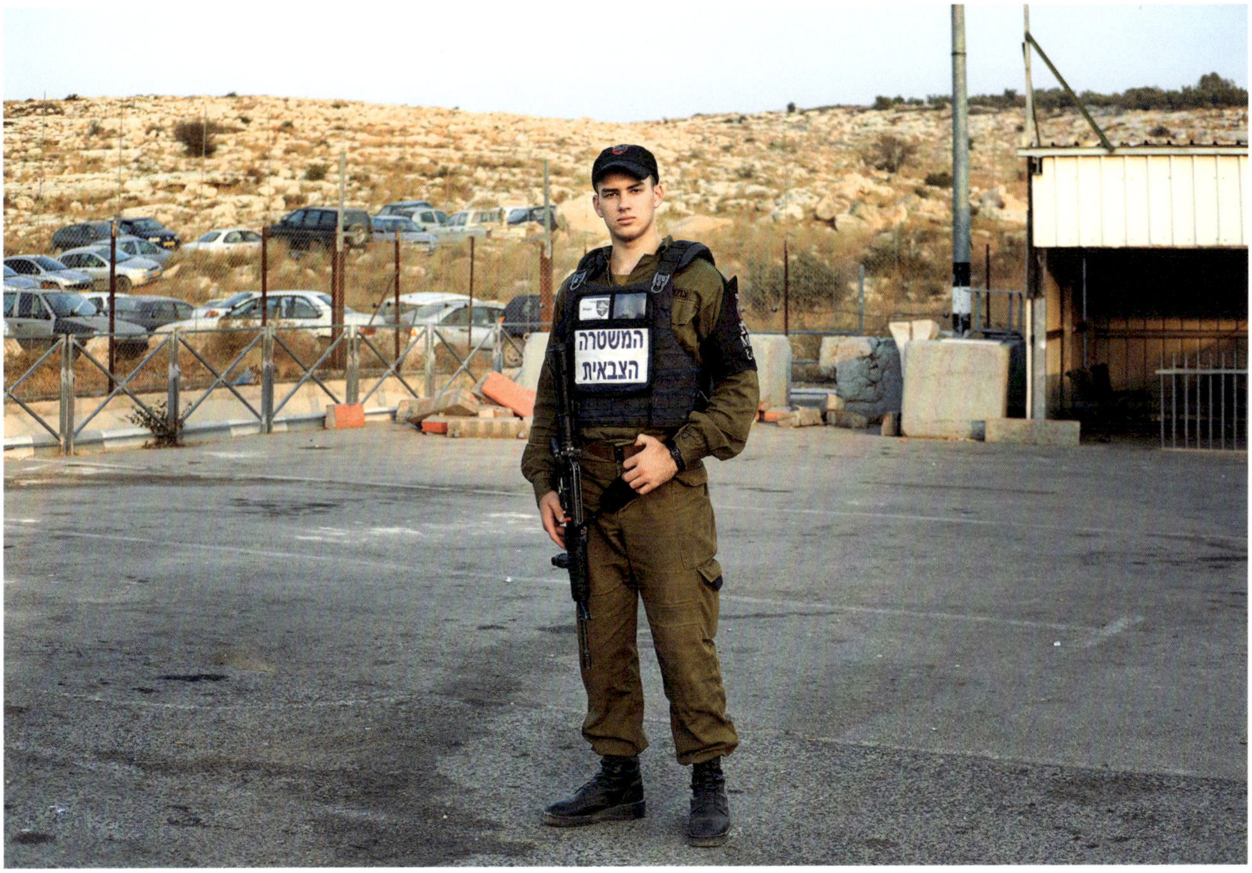
המשטרה
הצבאית

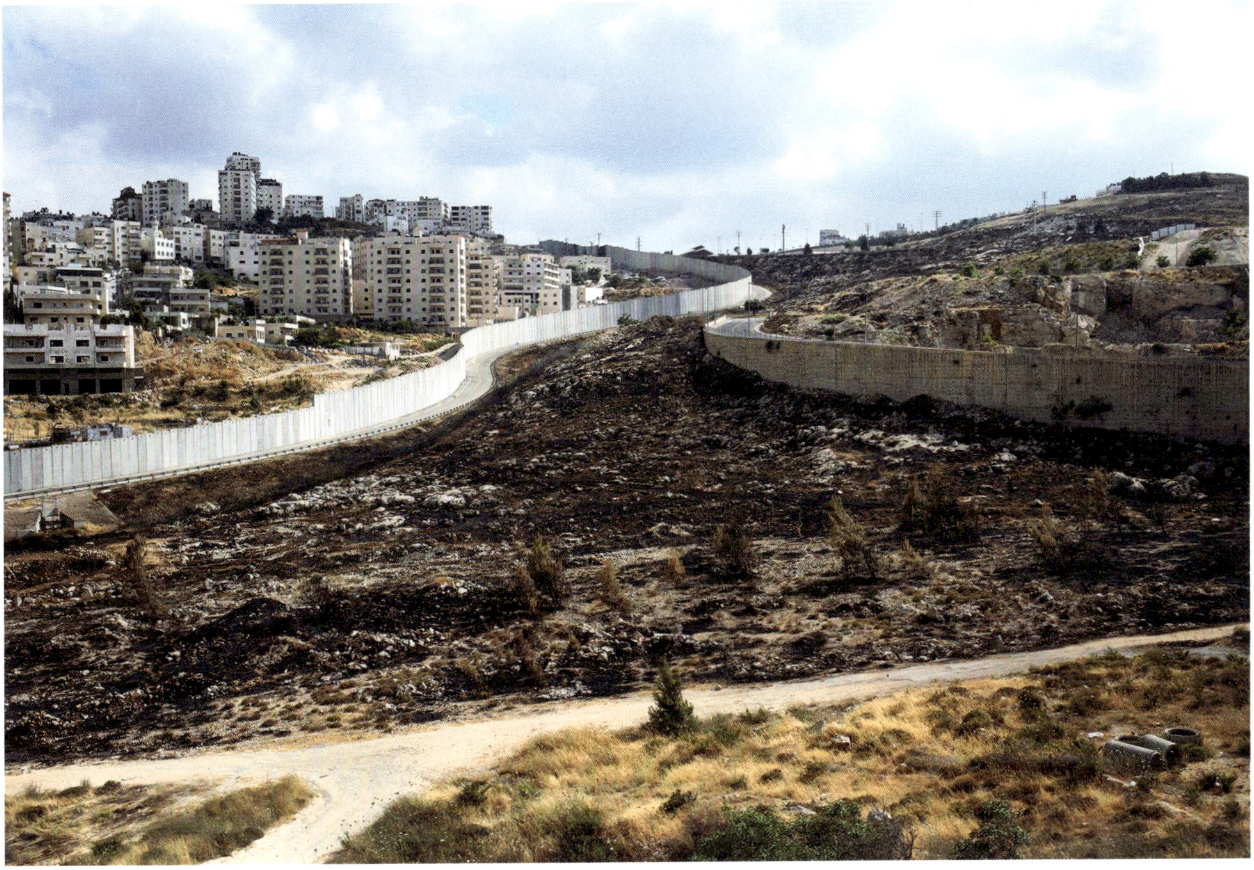

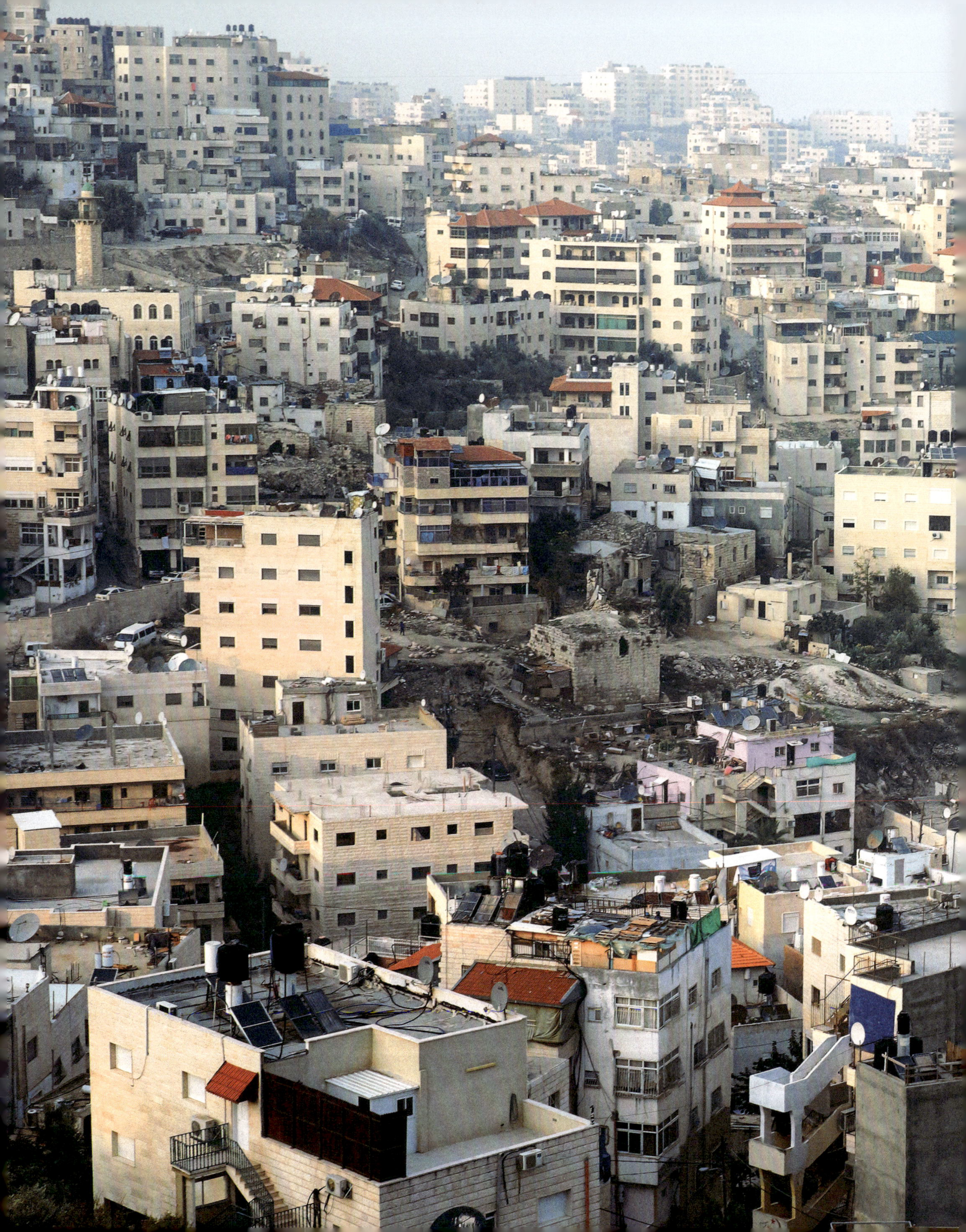

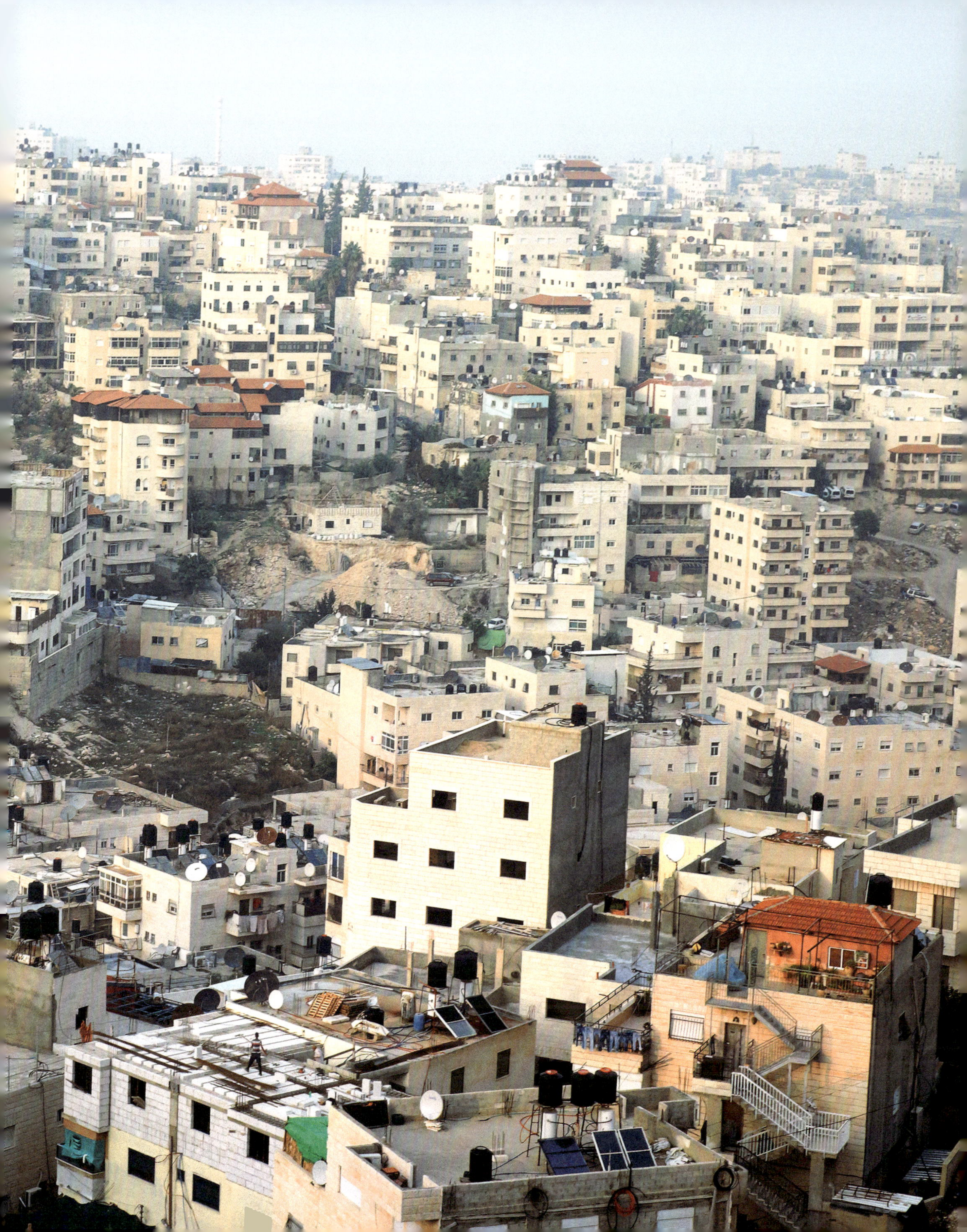

Josh | 22 | West Caldwell, New Jersey, USA | Infantry Platoon Commander

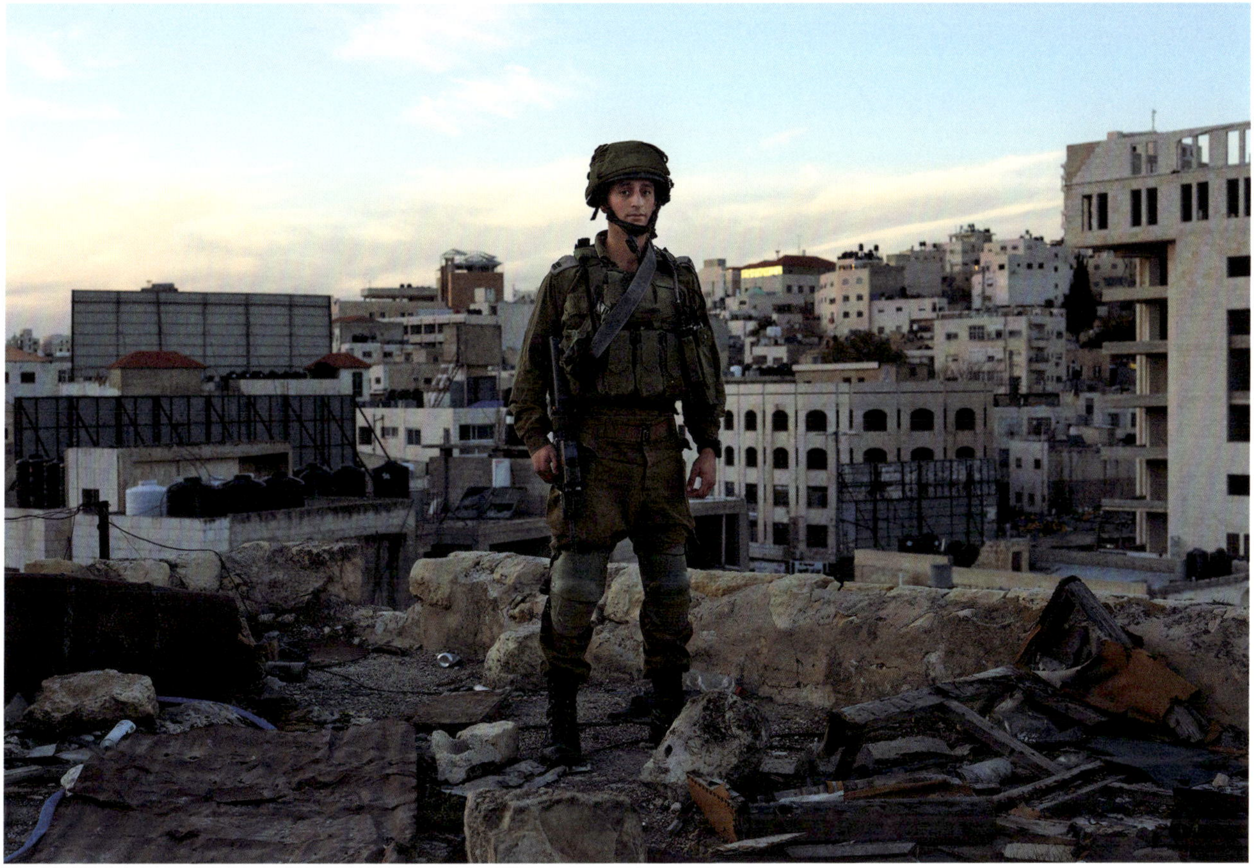

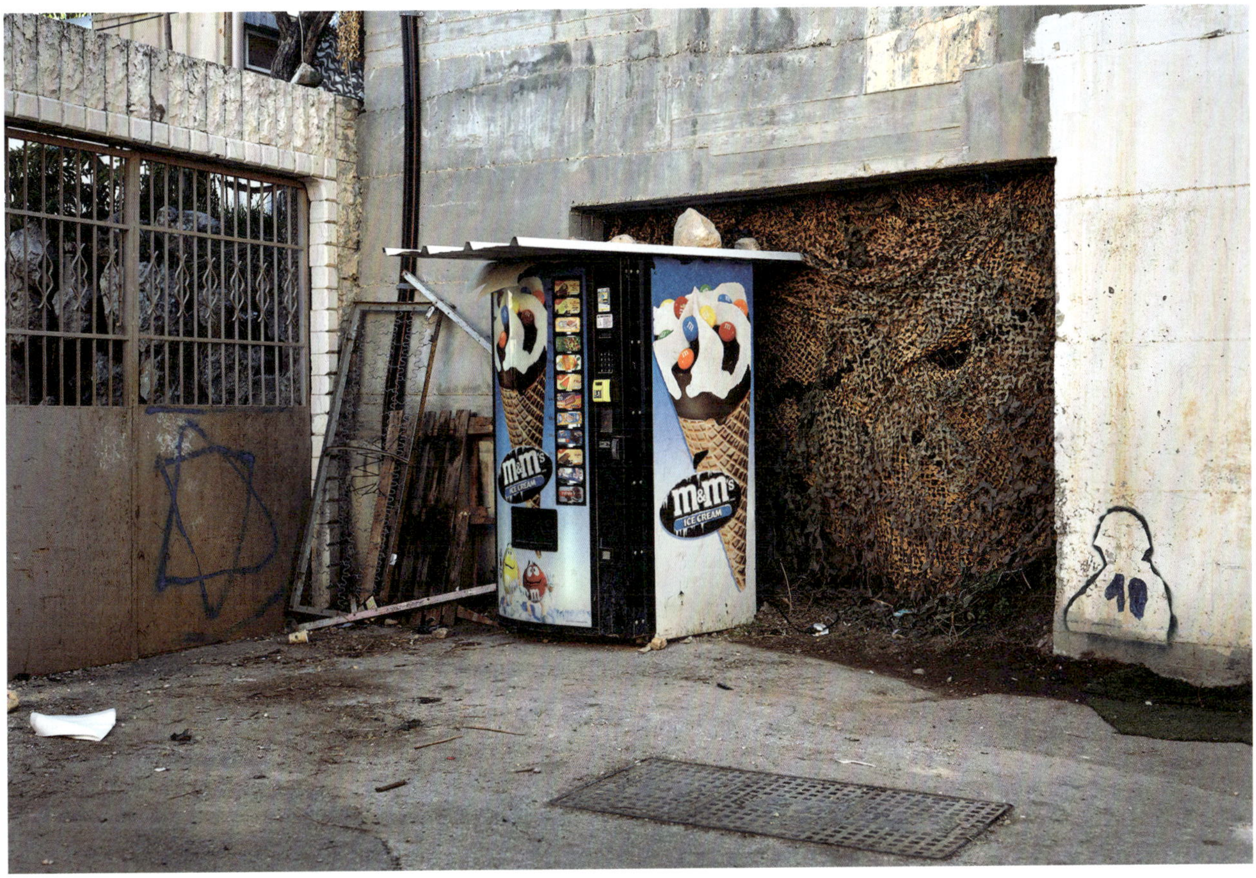
m&m's
ICE CREAM
m&m's
ICE CREAM

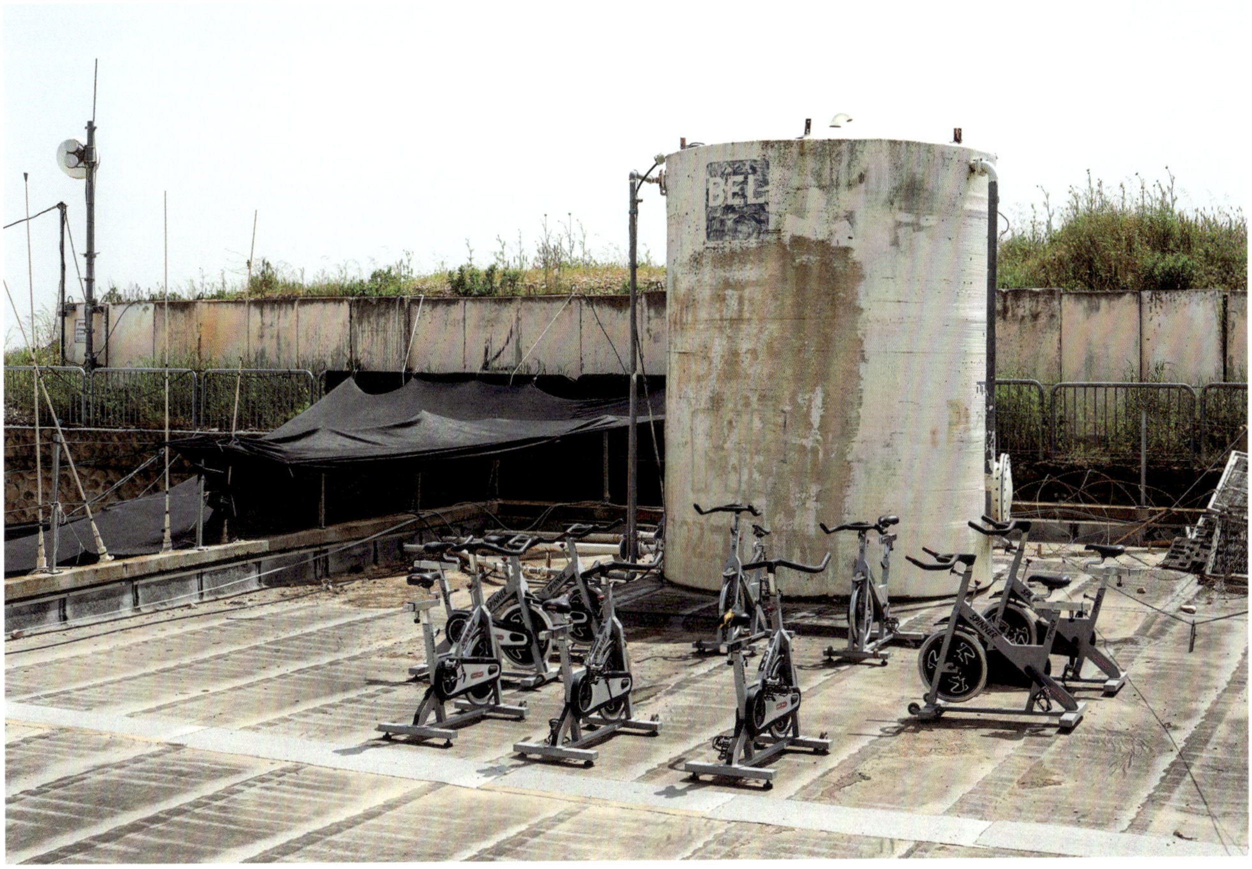
BEL

Hadar | 21 | Migdal Ha'Emek, Israel | Air Force Technician

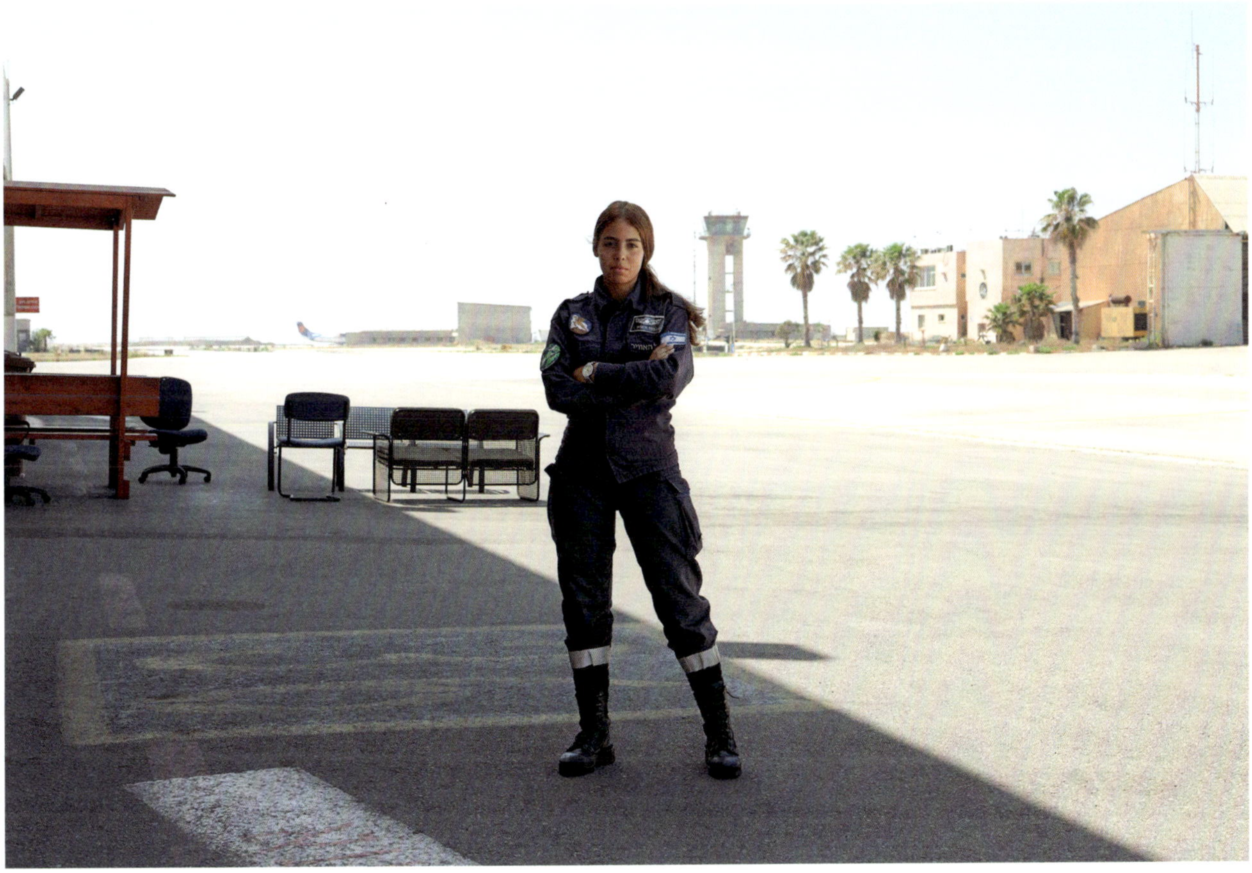

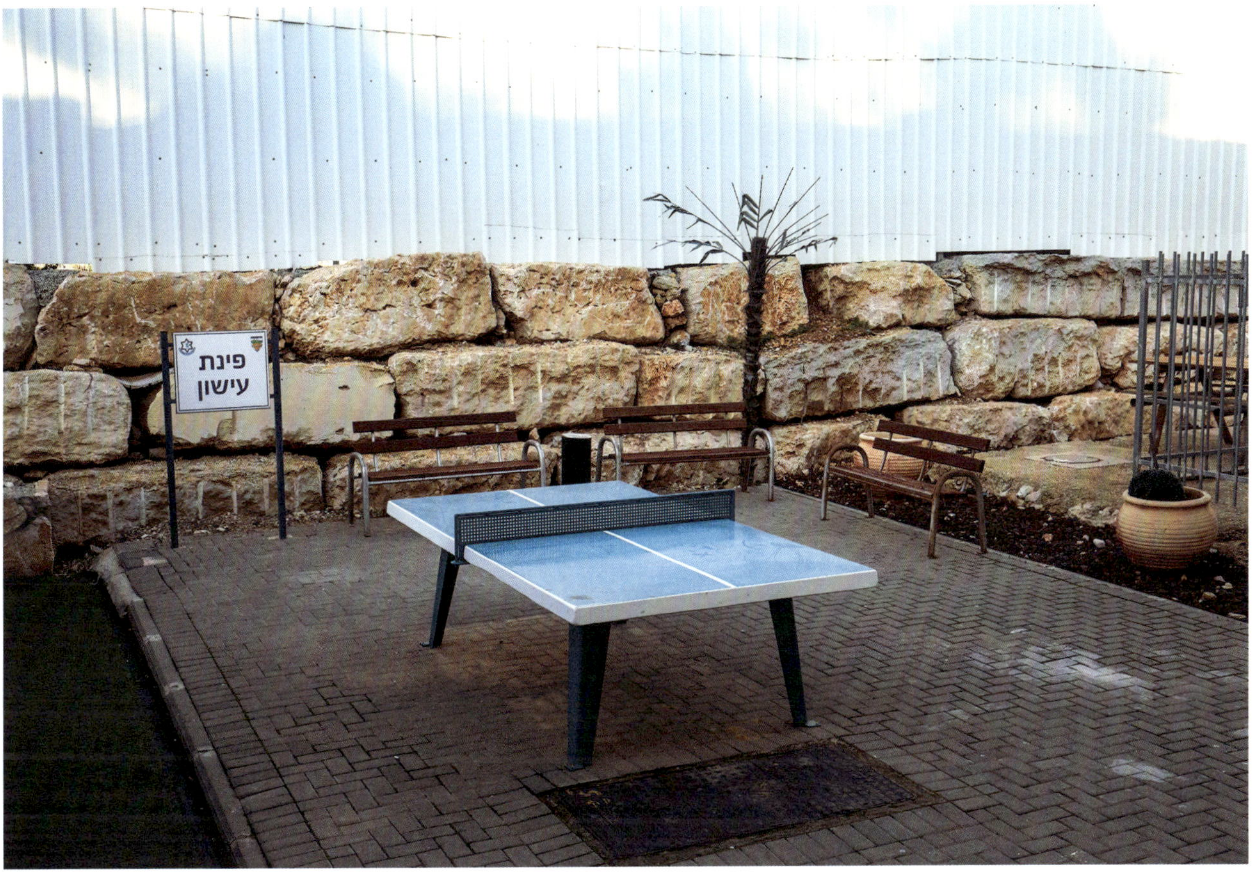
פינת
עישון

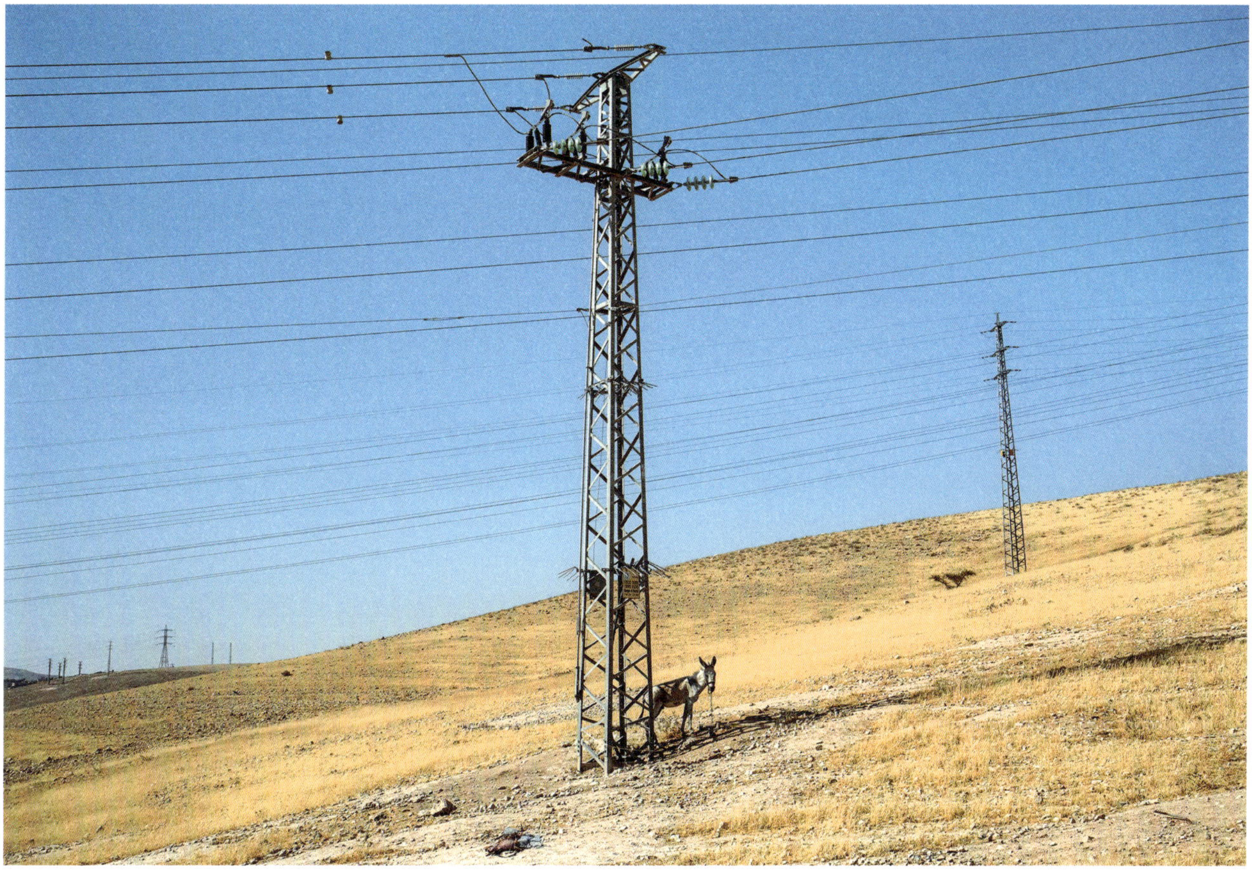

Raphael | 21 | Antwerp, Belgium | Infantry

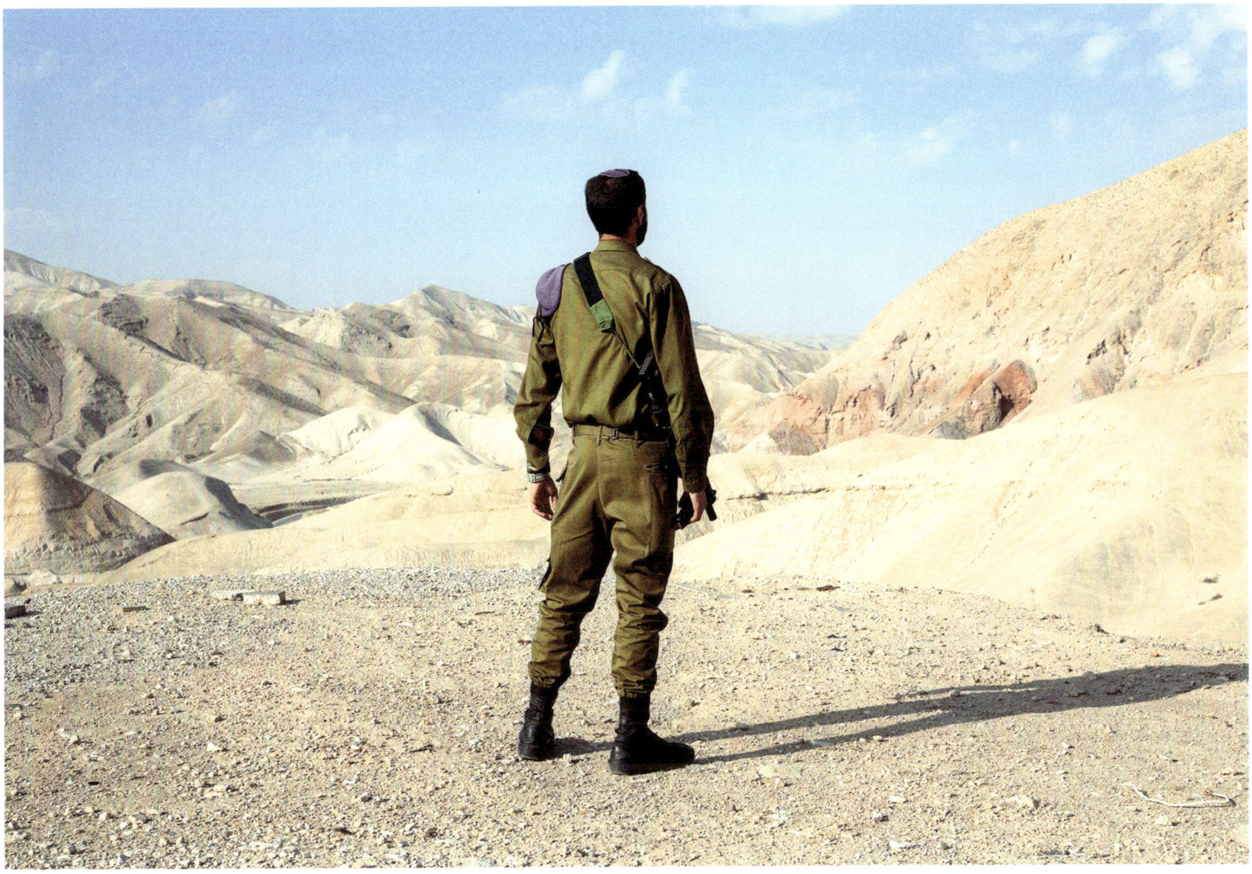

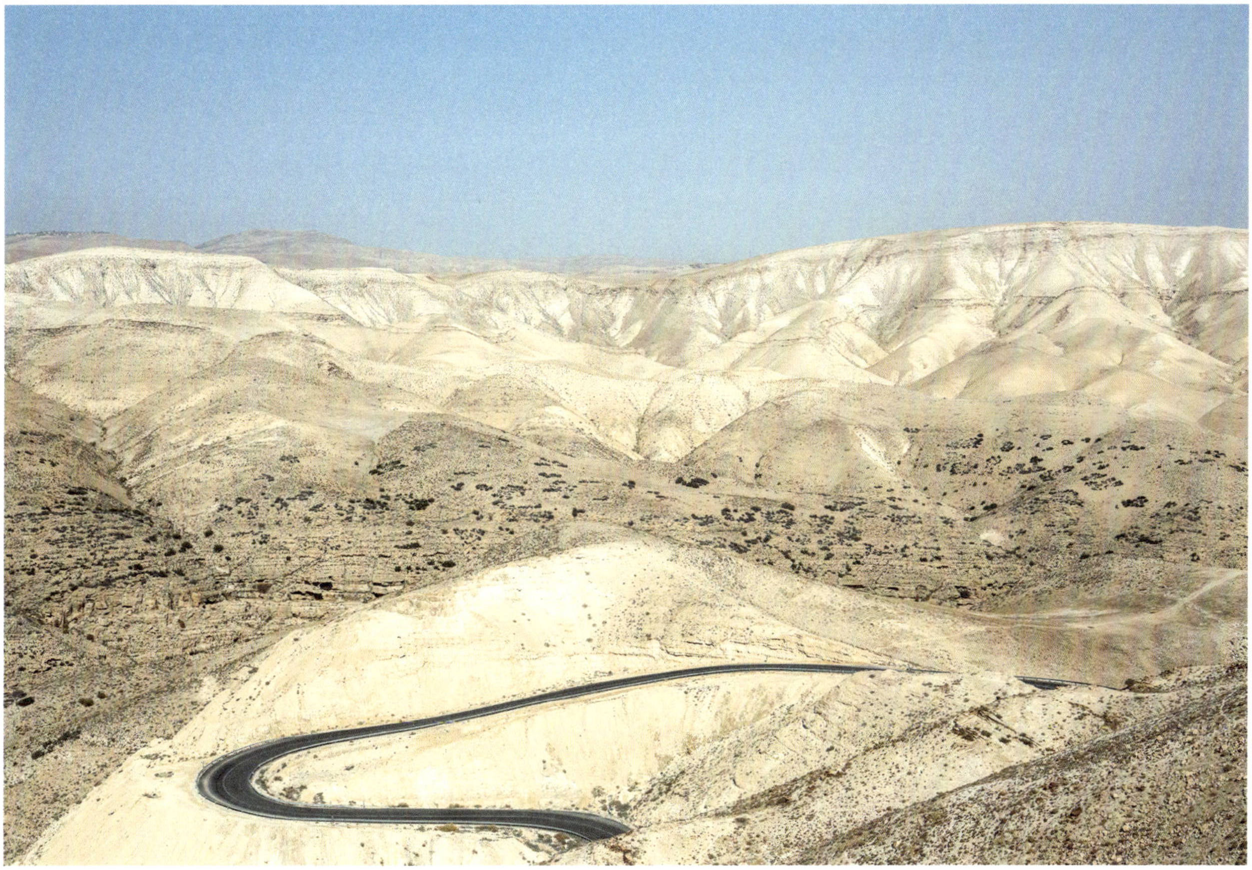

Julien | 21 | Edmonton, Alberta, Canada | Infantry

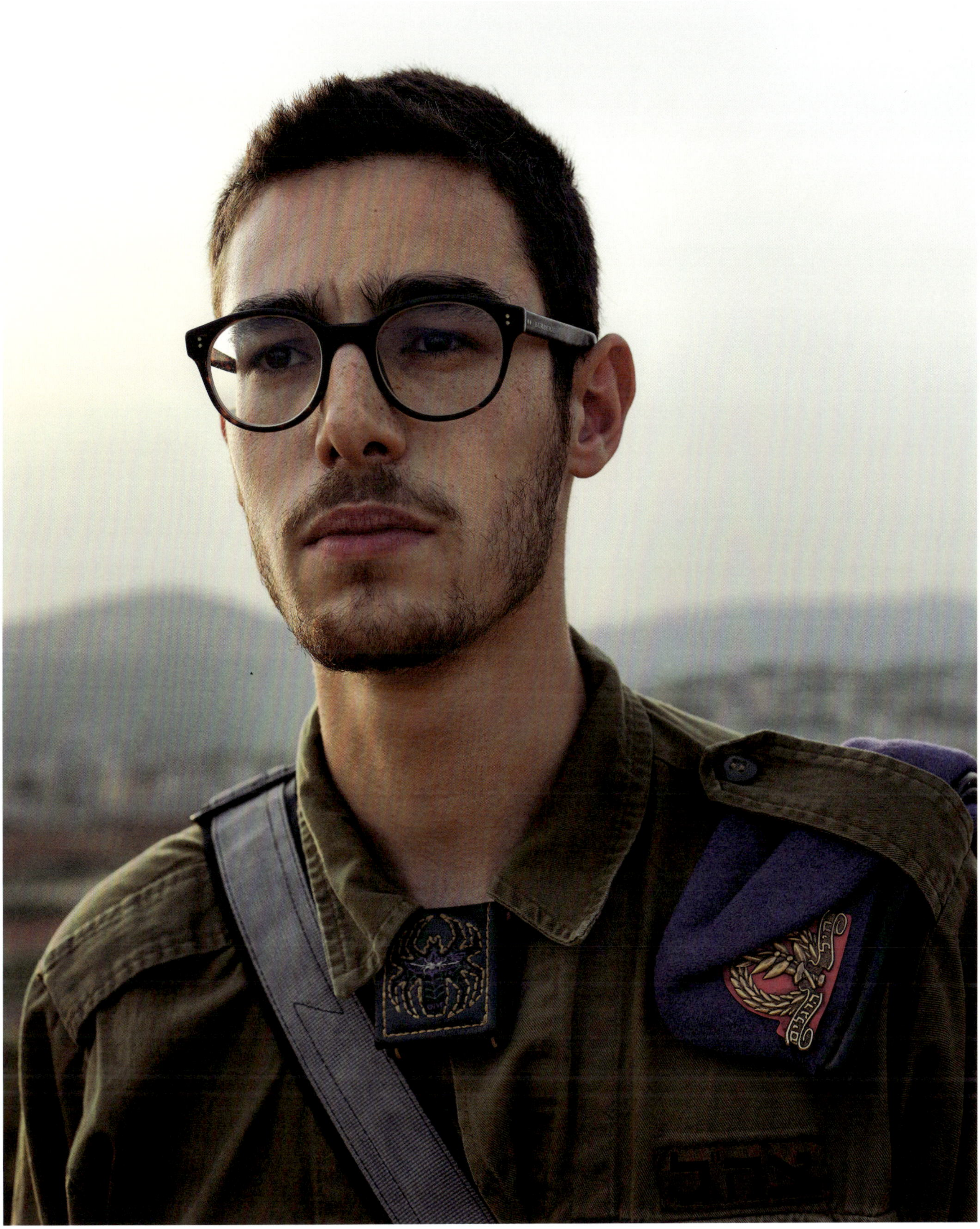

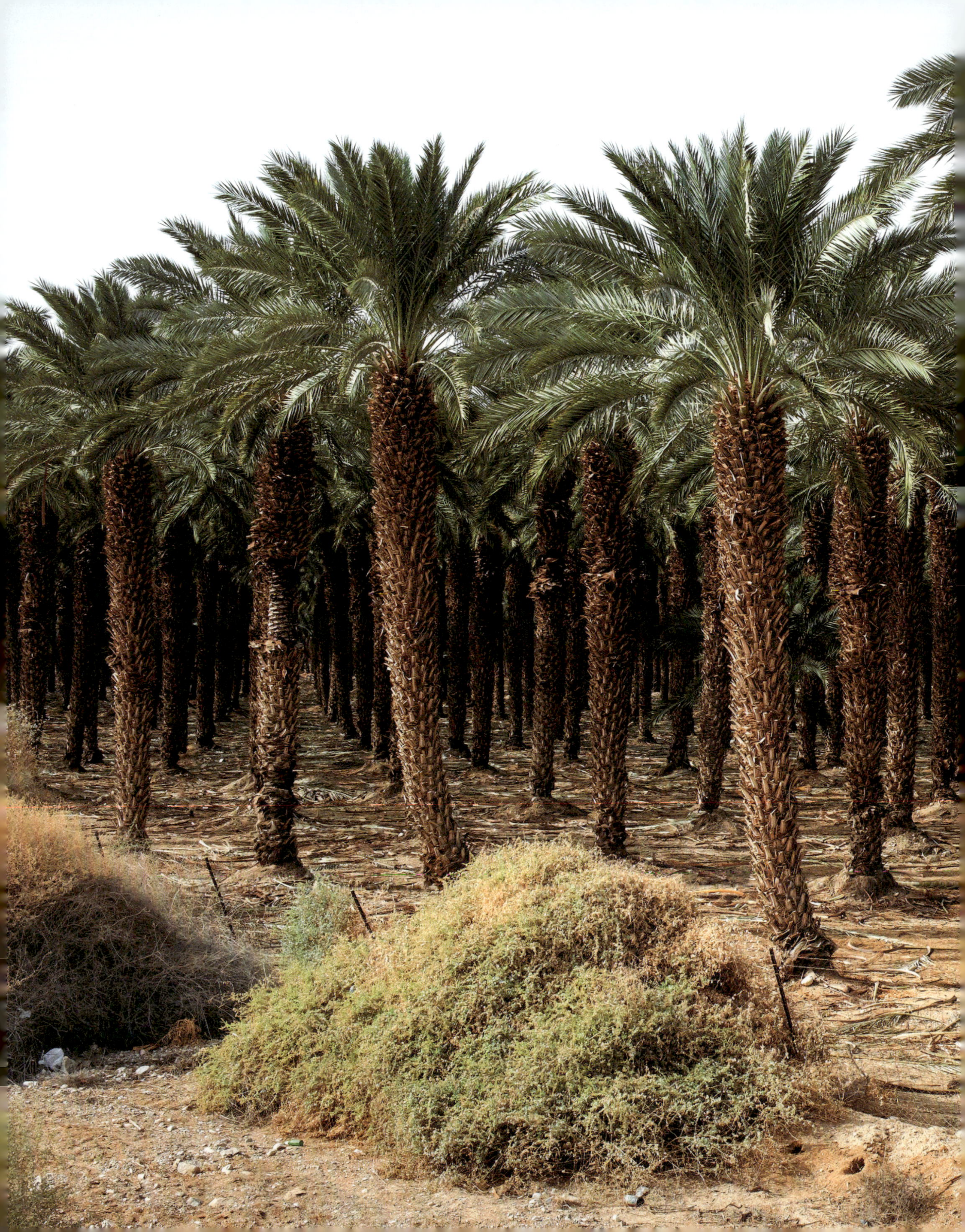

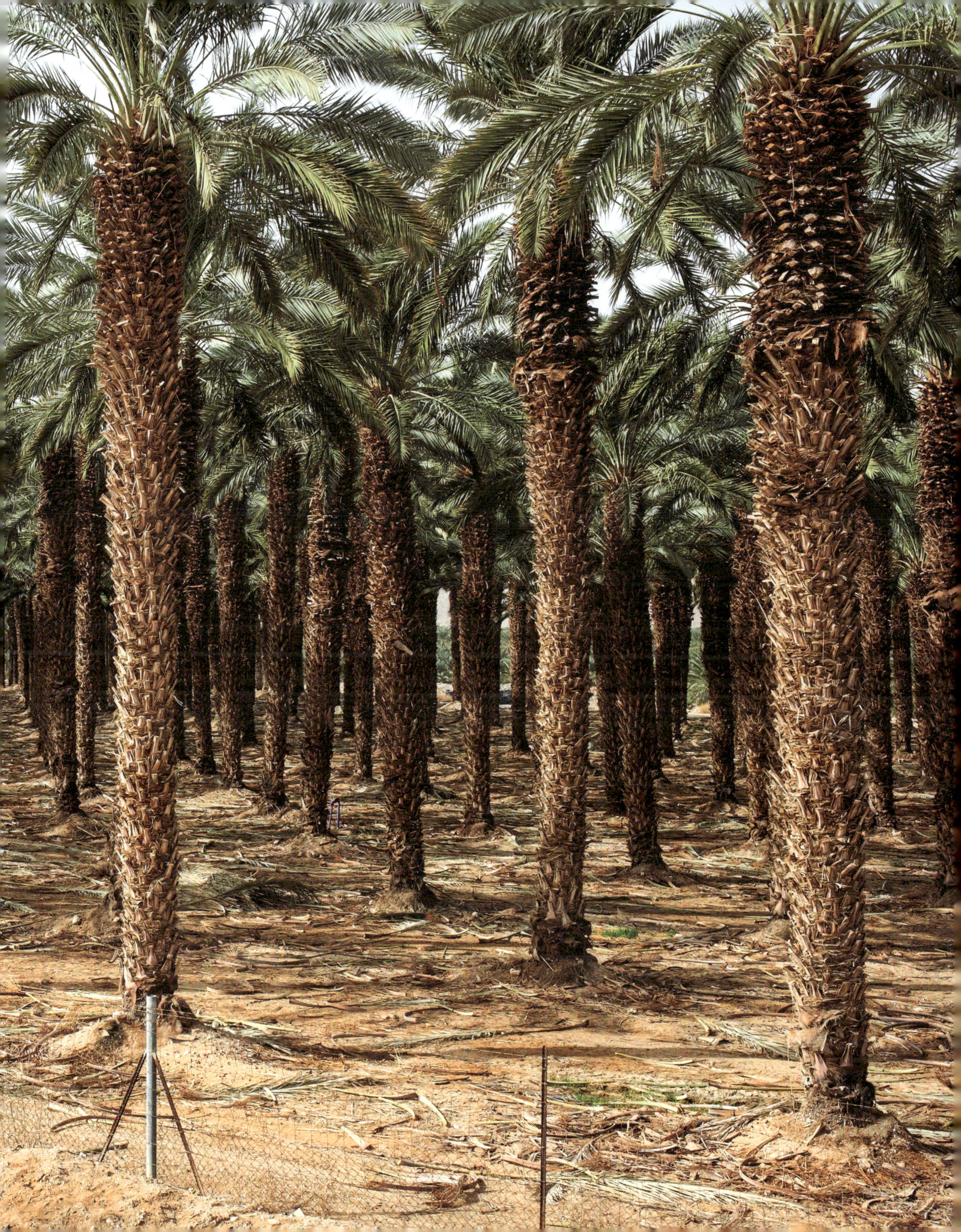

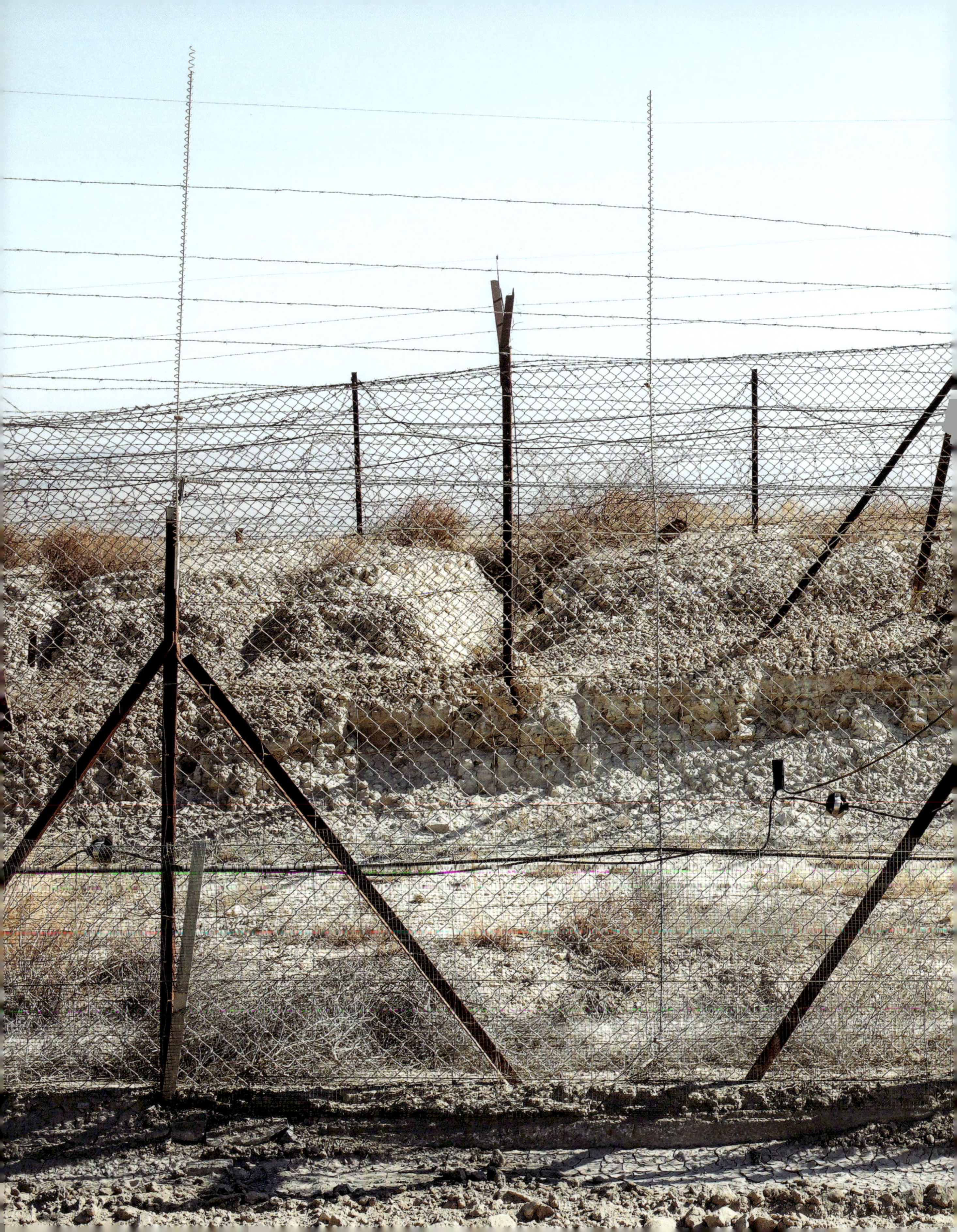

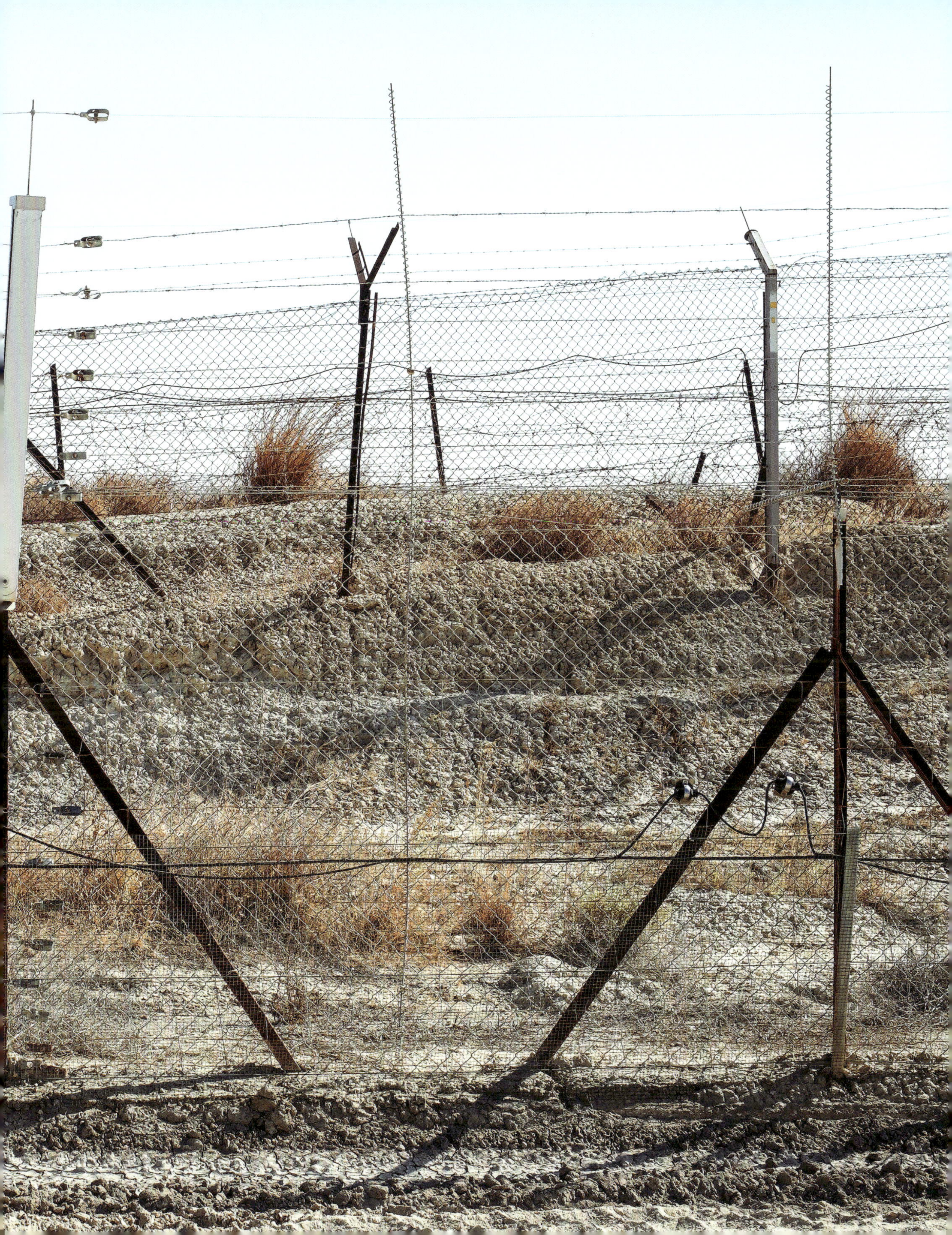

Niv | 19 | Panama City, Panama | Paratrooper

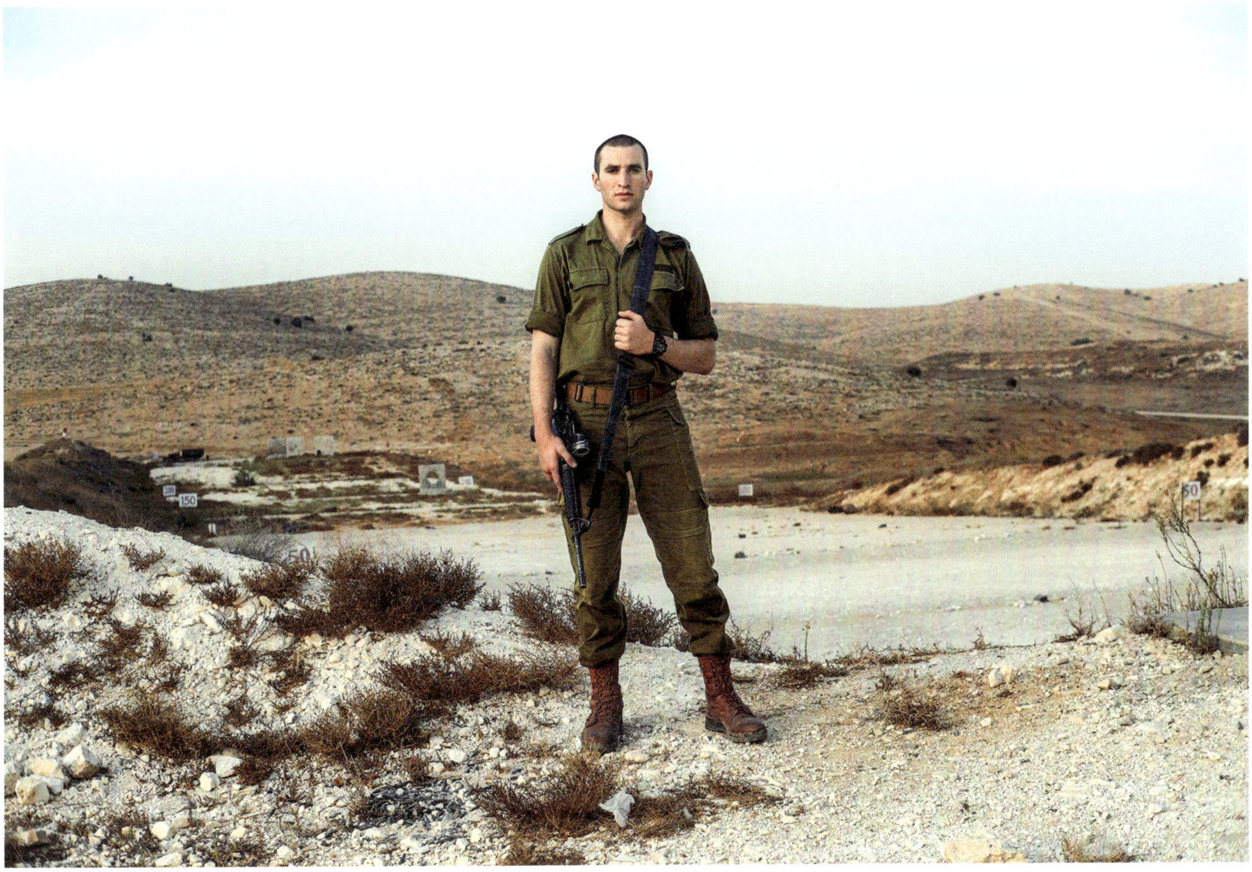

Daniel | 21 | São Paulo, Brazil | Paratrooper

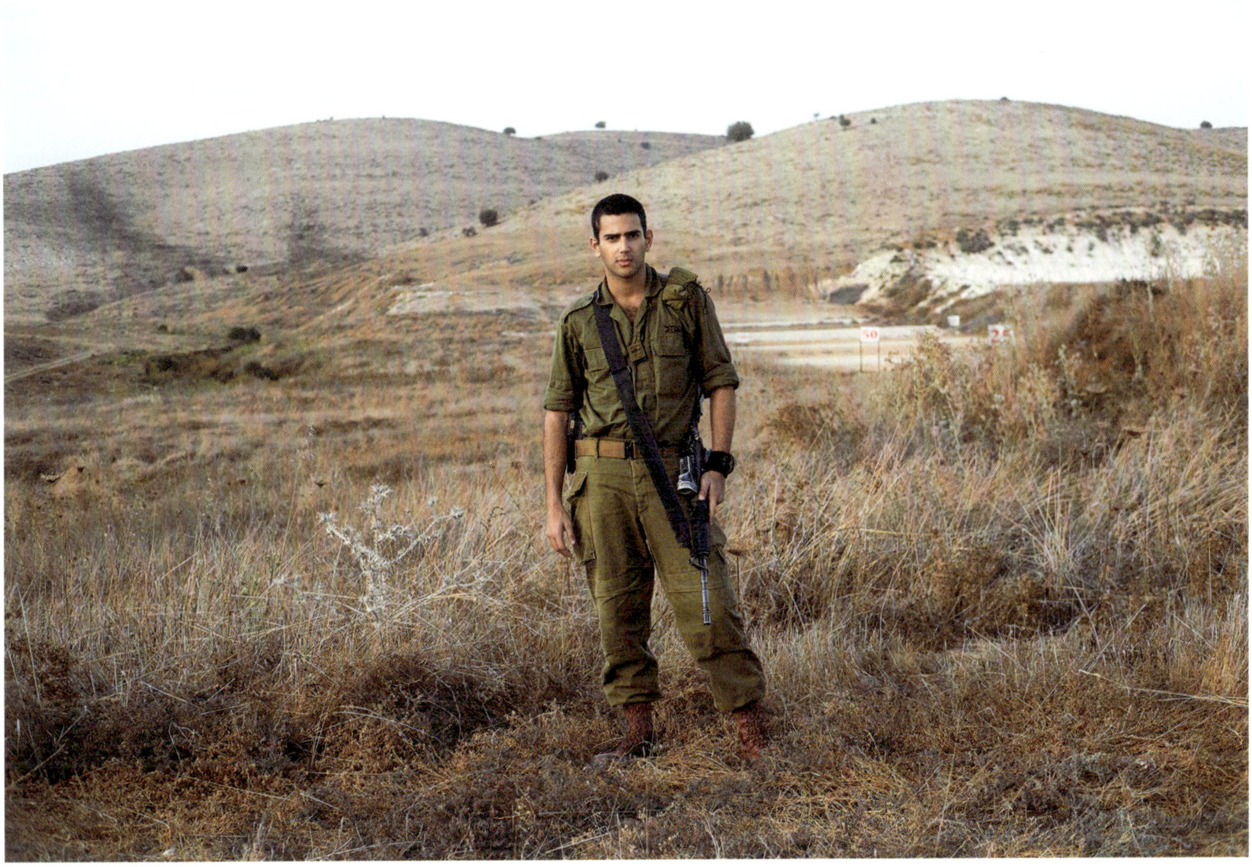

Matthias | 23 | Paris, France | Paratrooper

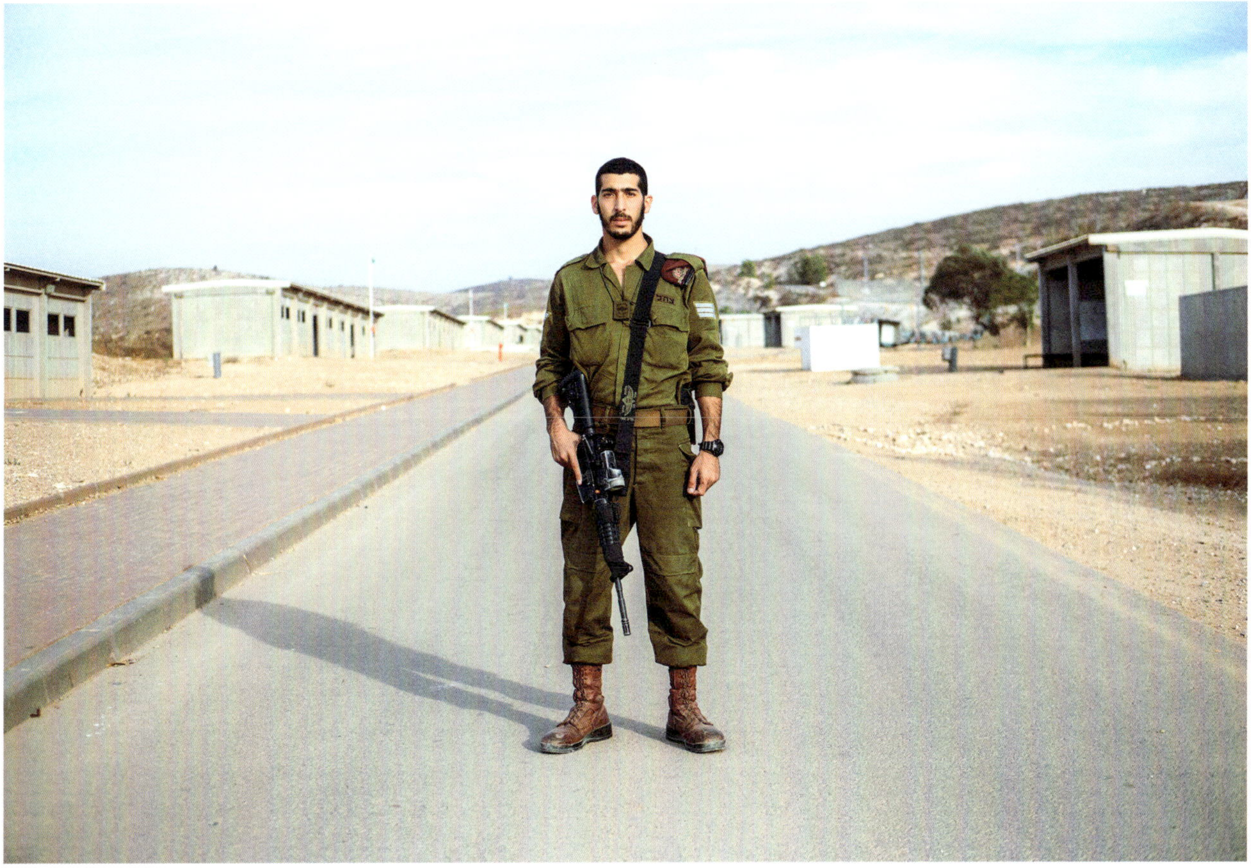

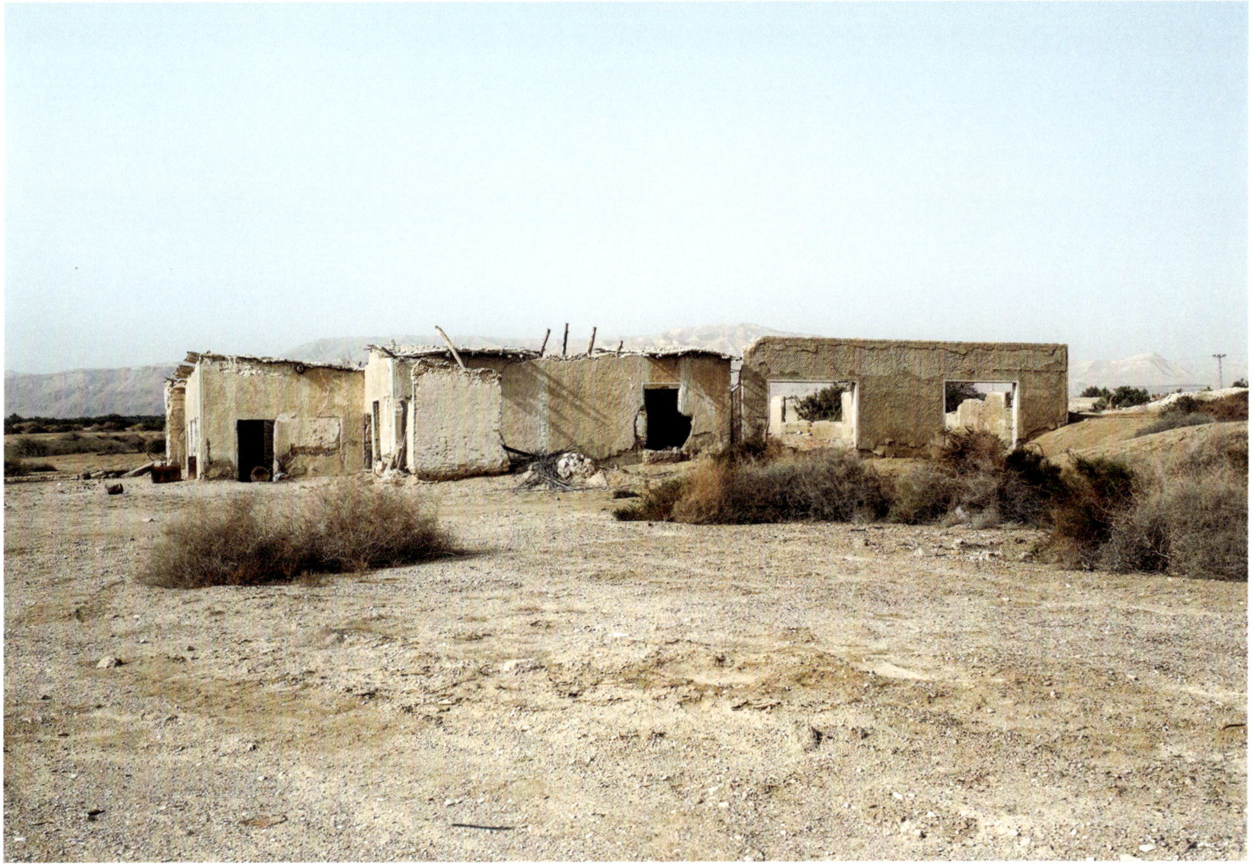

Samuel | 19 | Milan, Italy | Infantry

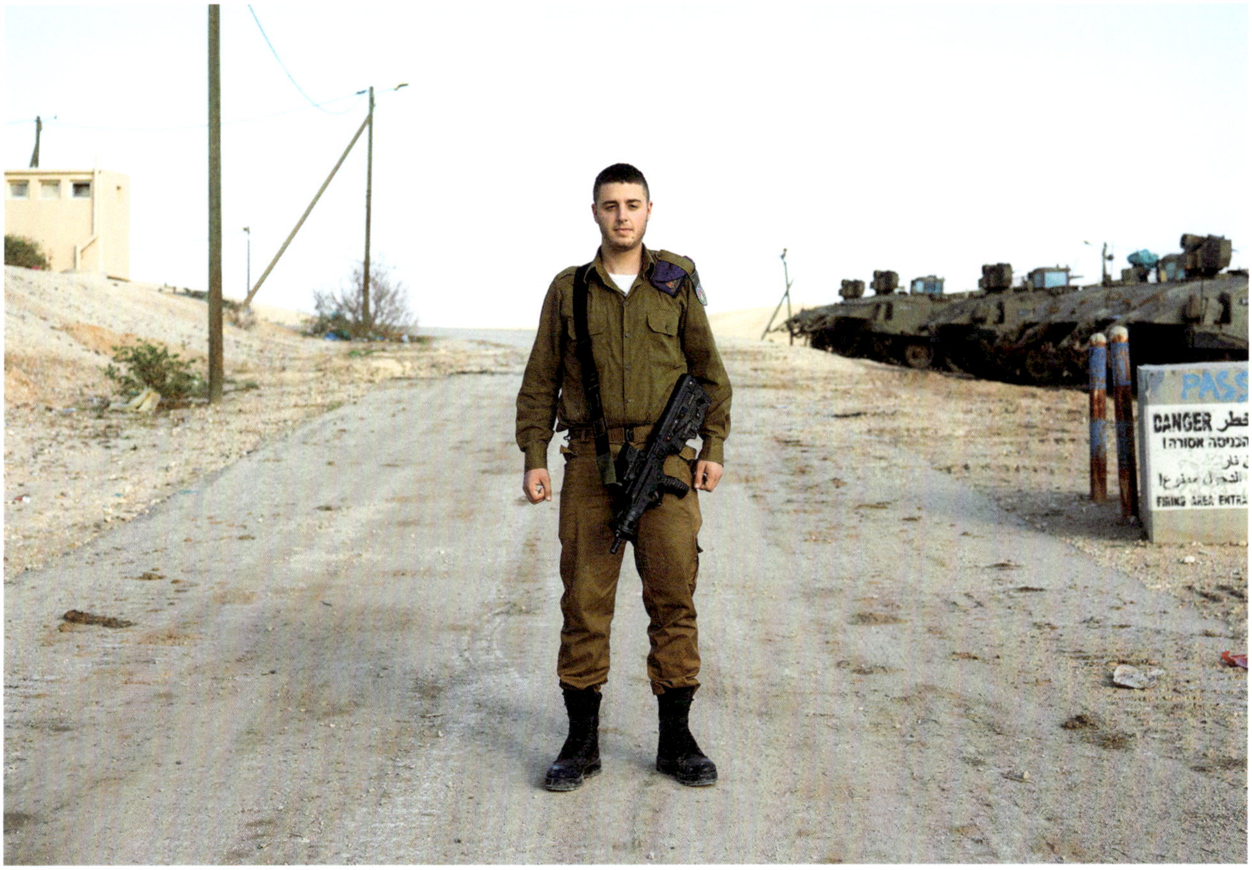
DANGER
הכניסה אסורה!

Daniel | 23 | Meghalaya, India | Armoured Brigade

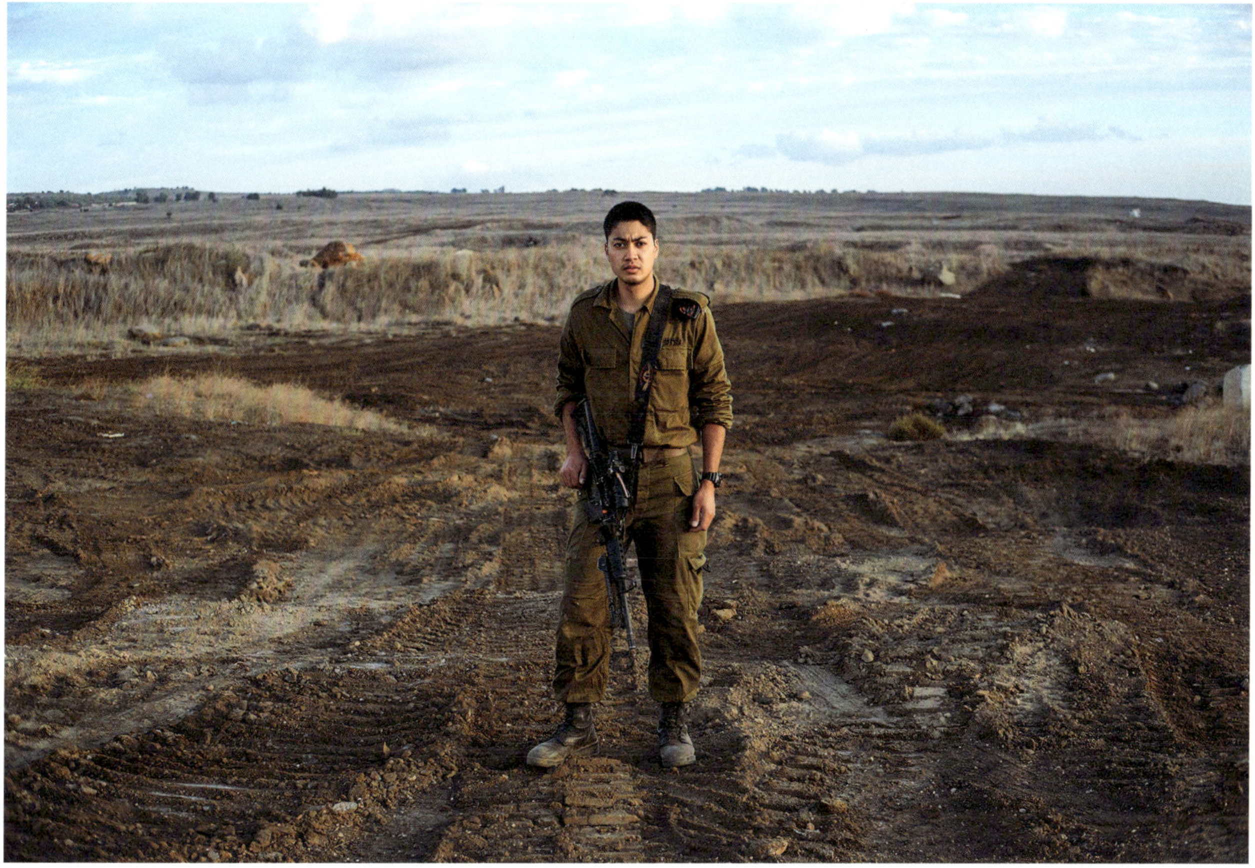

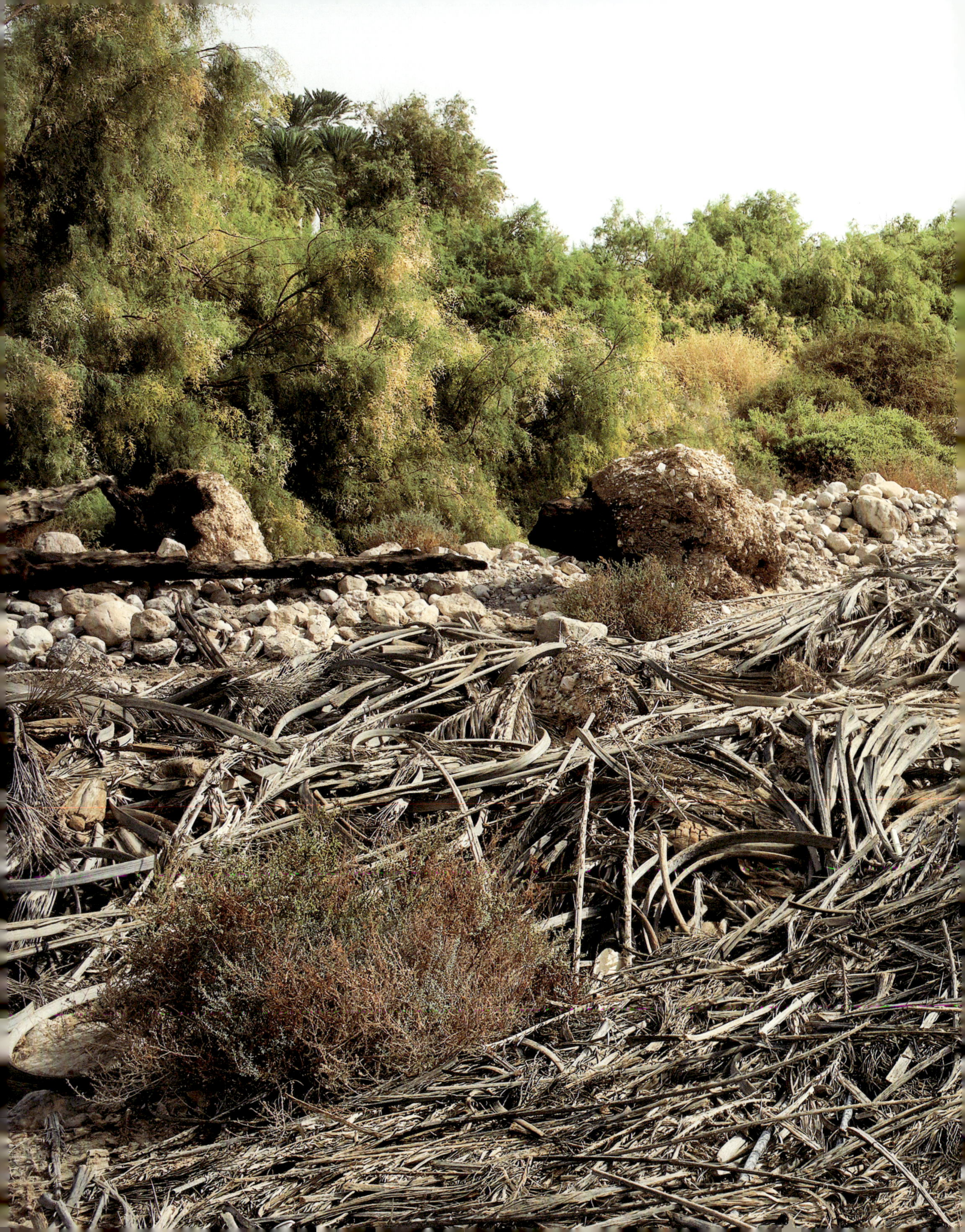

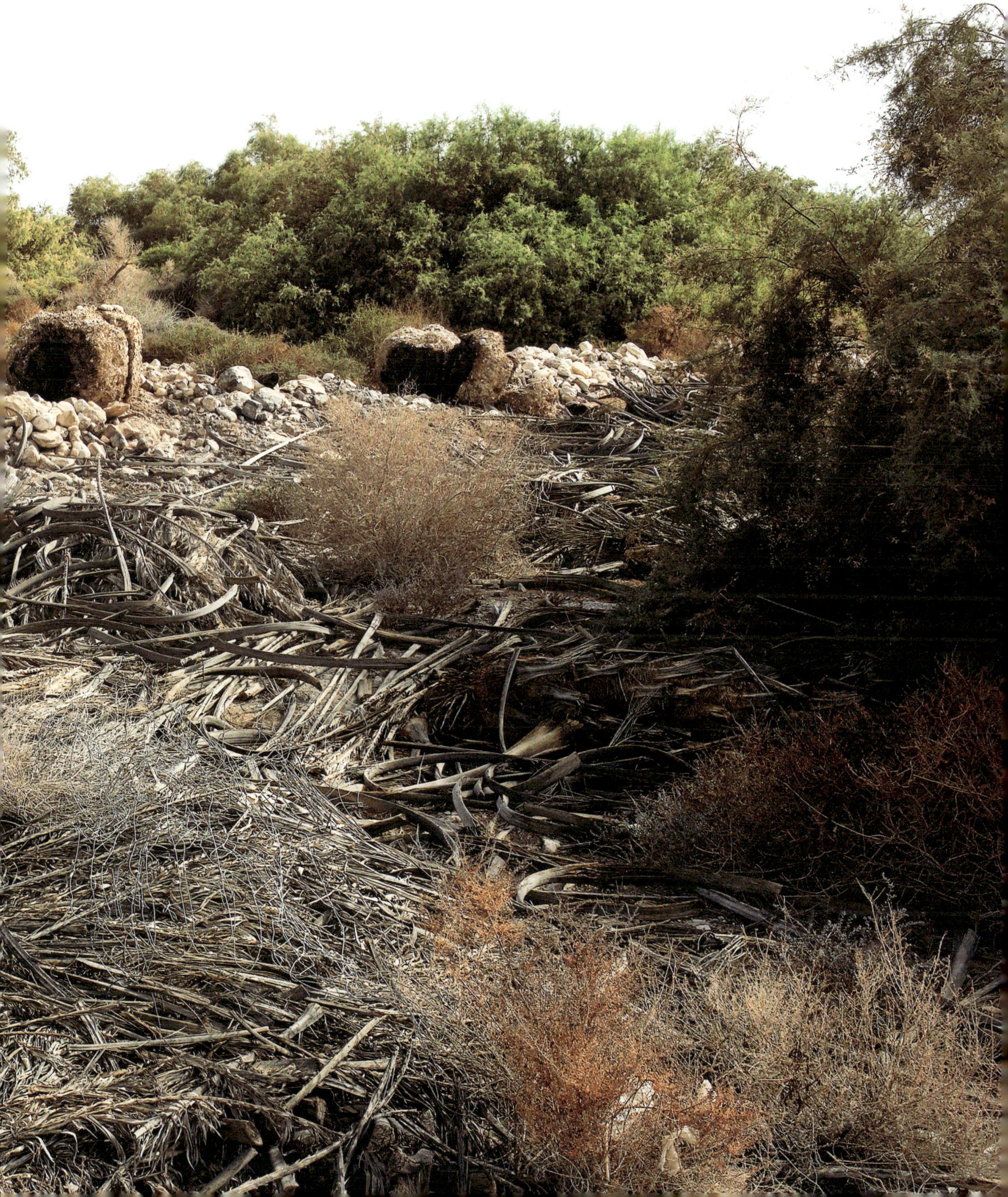

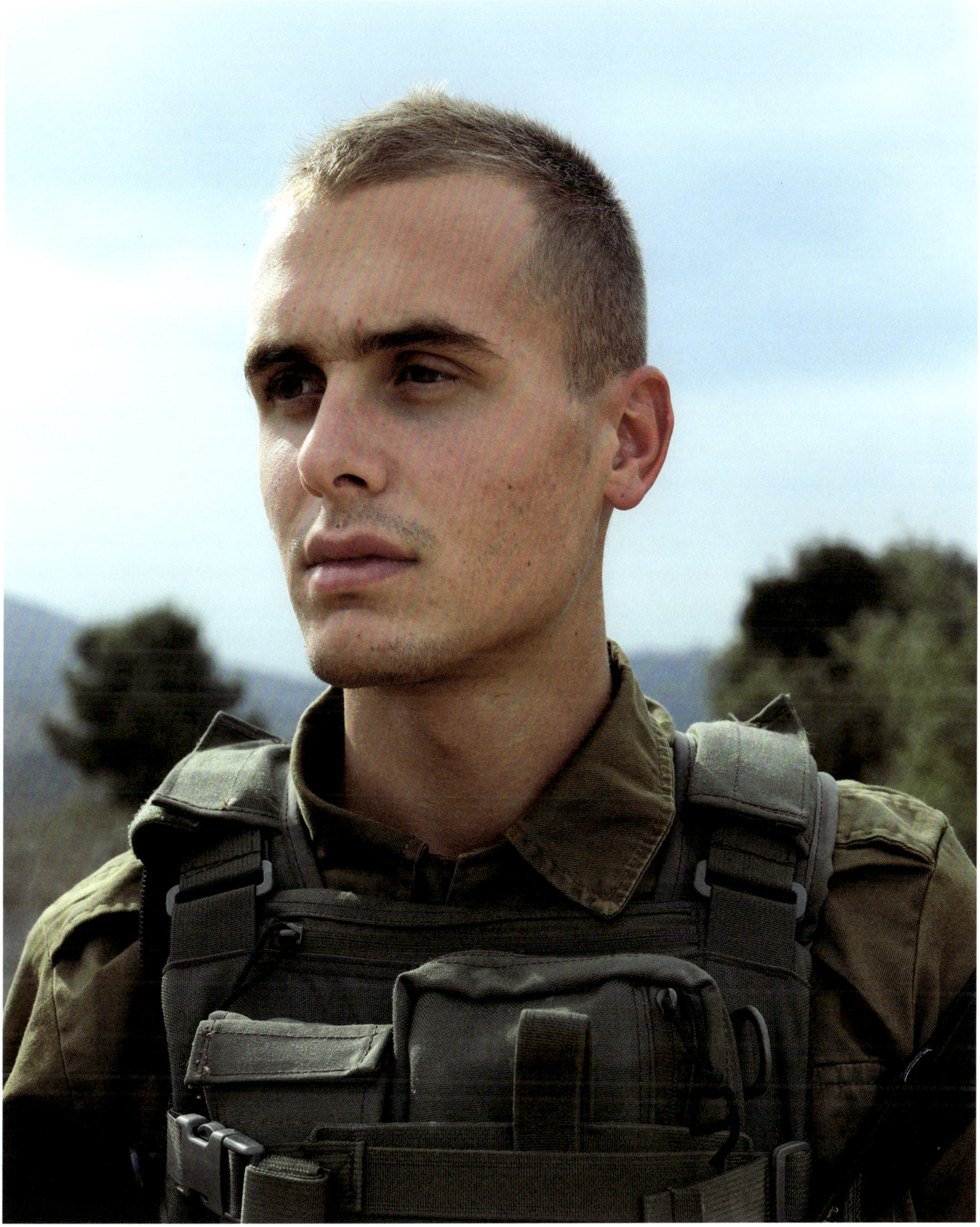

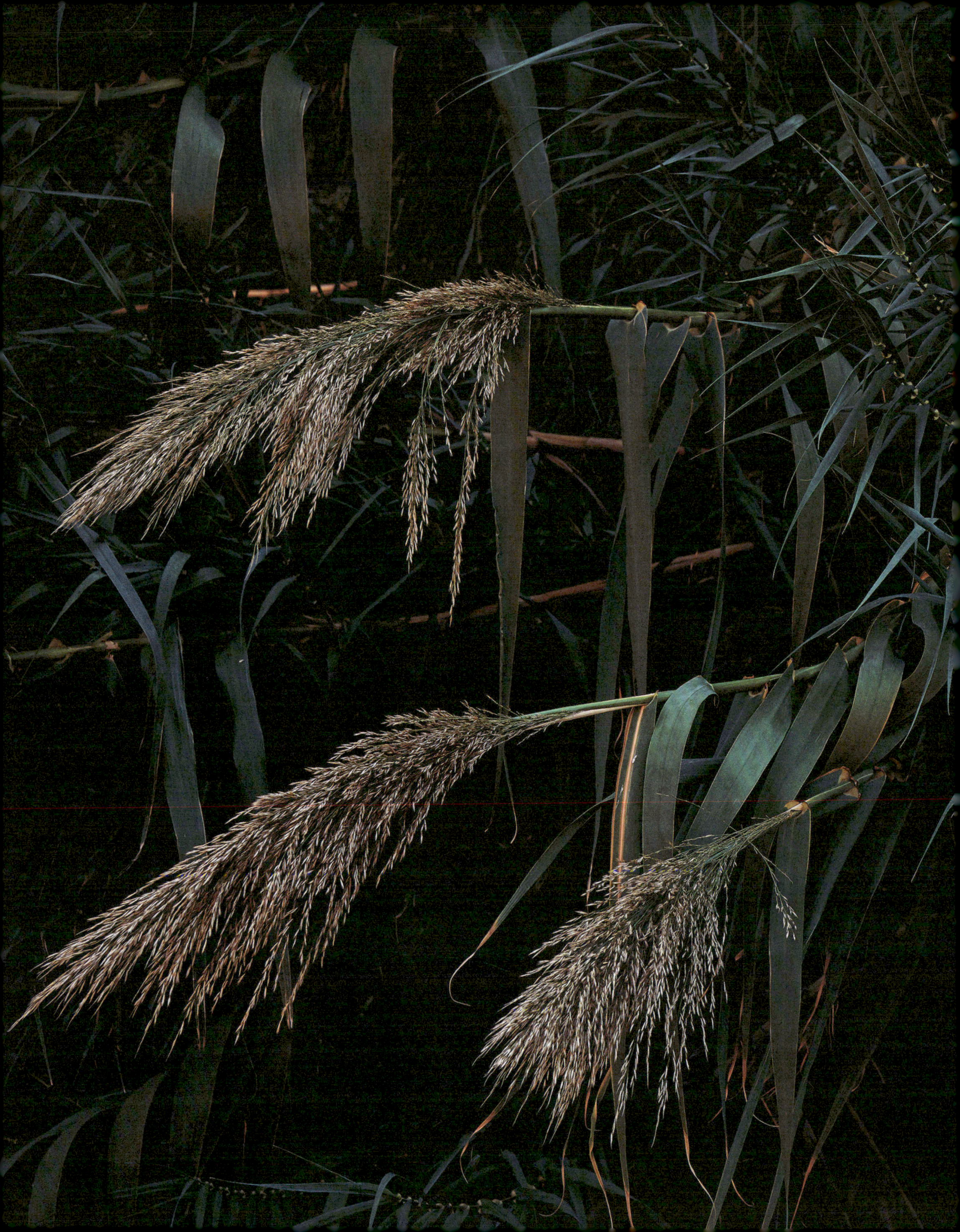

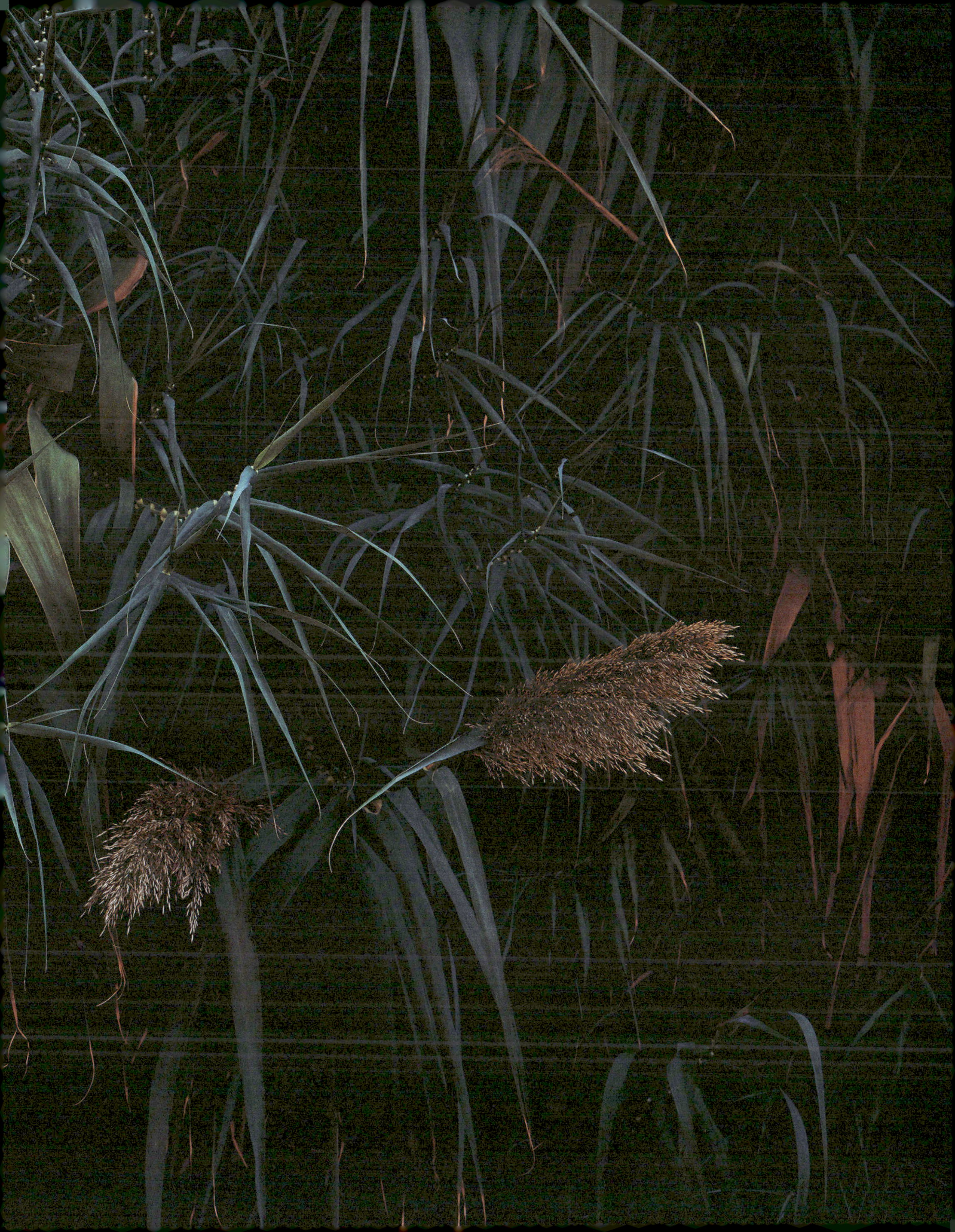

Igor | 21 | Magnitogorsk, Russia | Search and Rescue

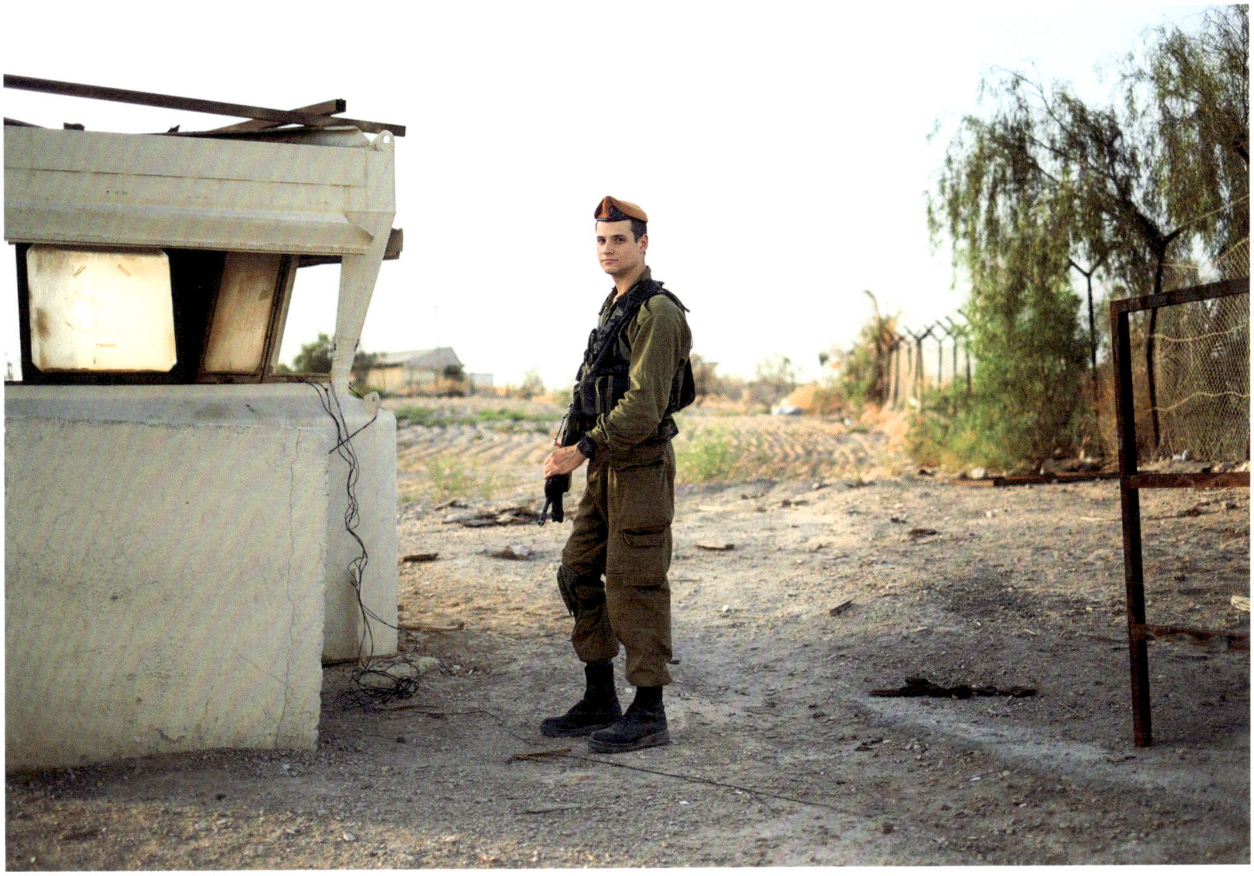

Yael | 21 | Pleasanton, California, USA | Search and Rescue

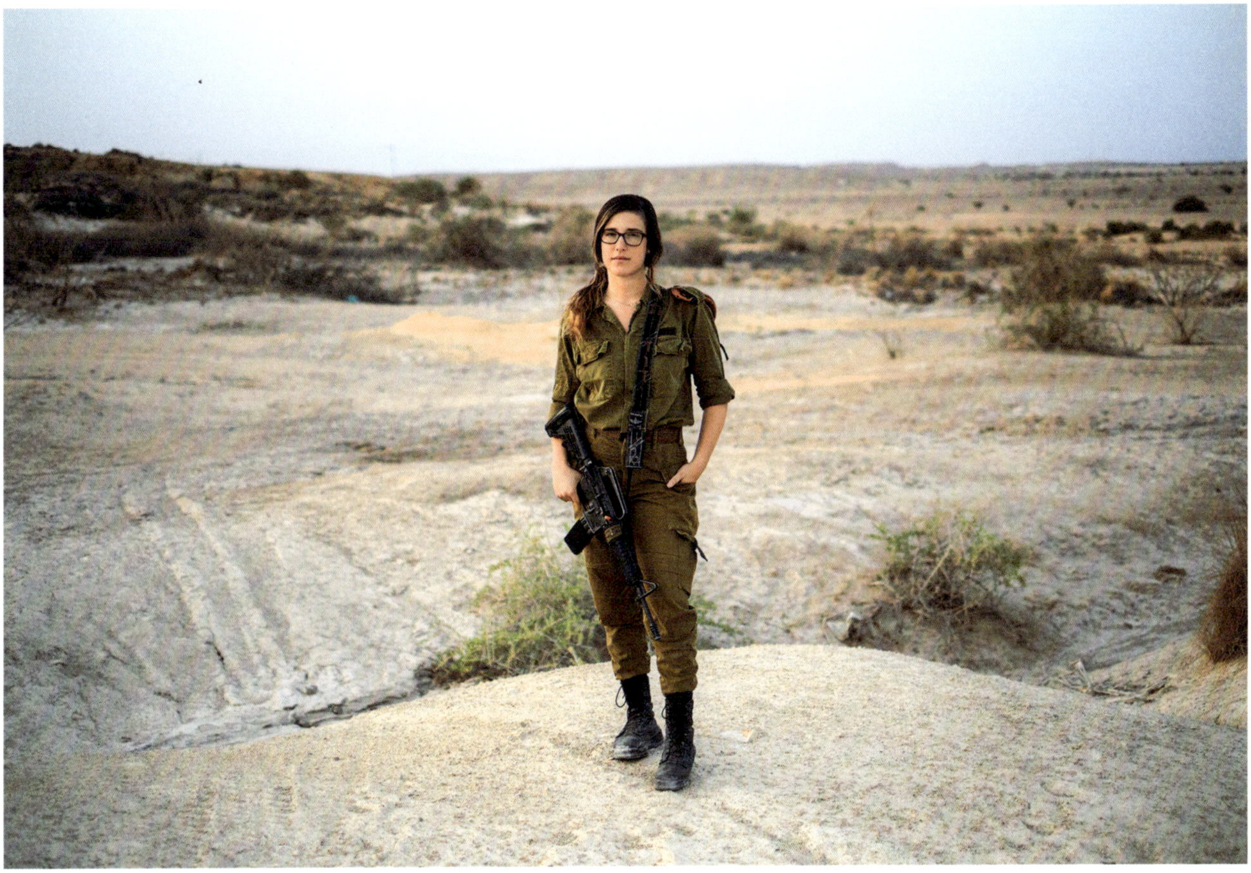

Nikita | 21 | Barnaul, Russia | Search and Rescue

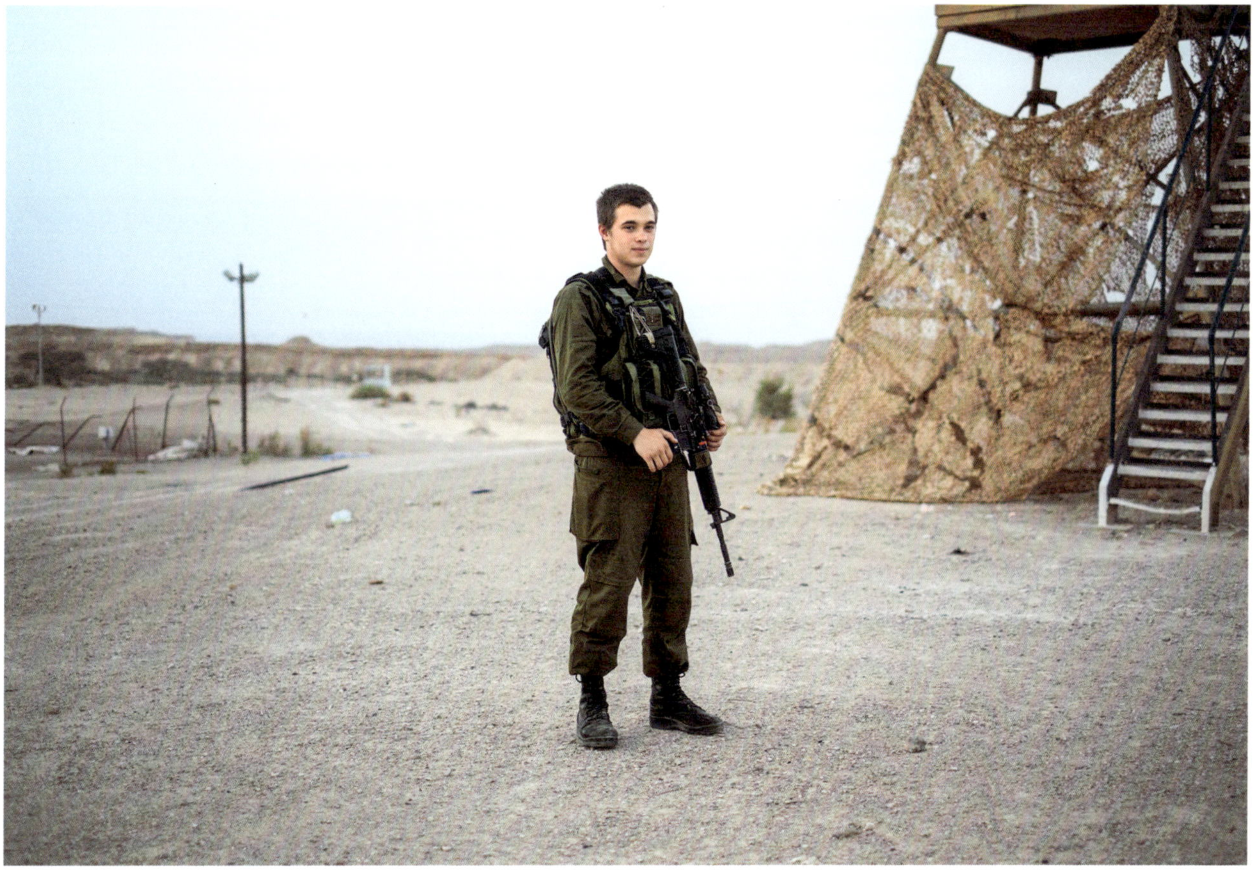

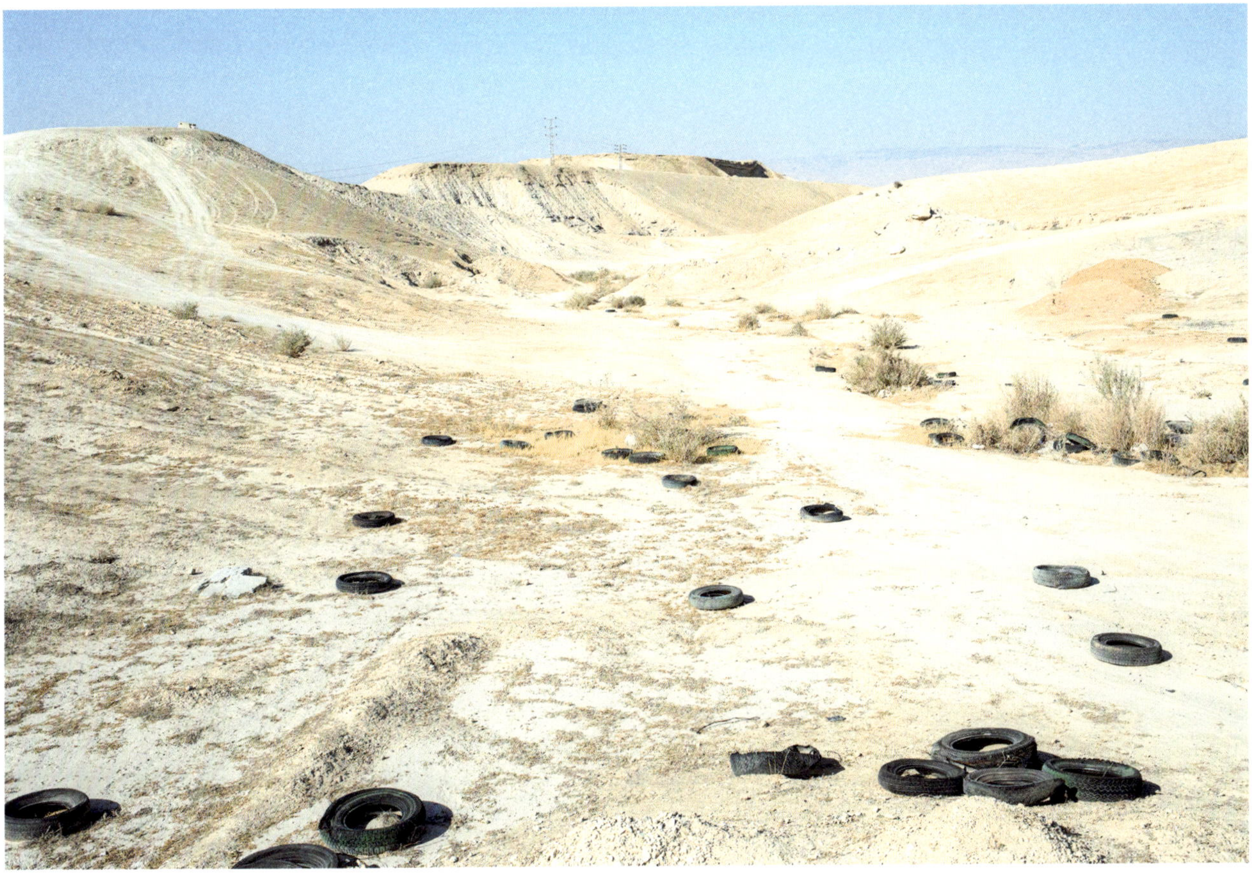

Eli | 20 | Rostov, Russia | Infantry

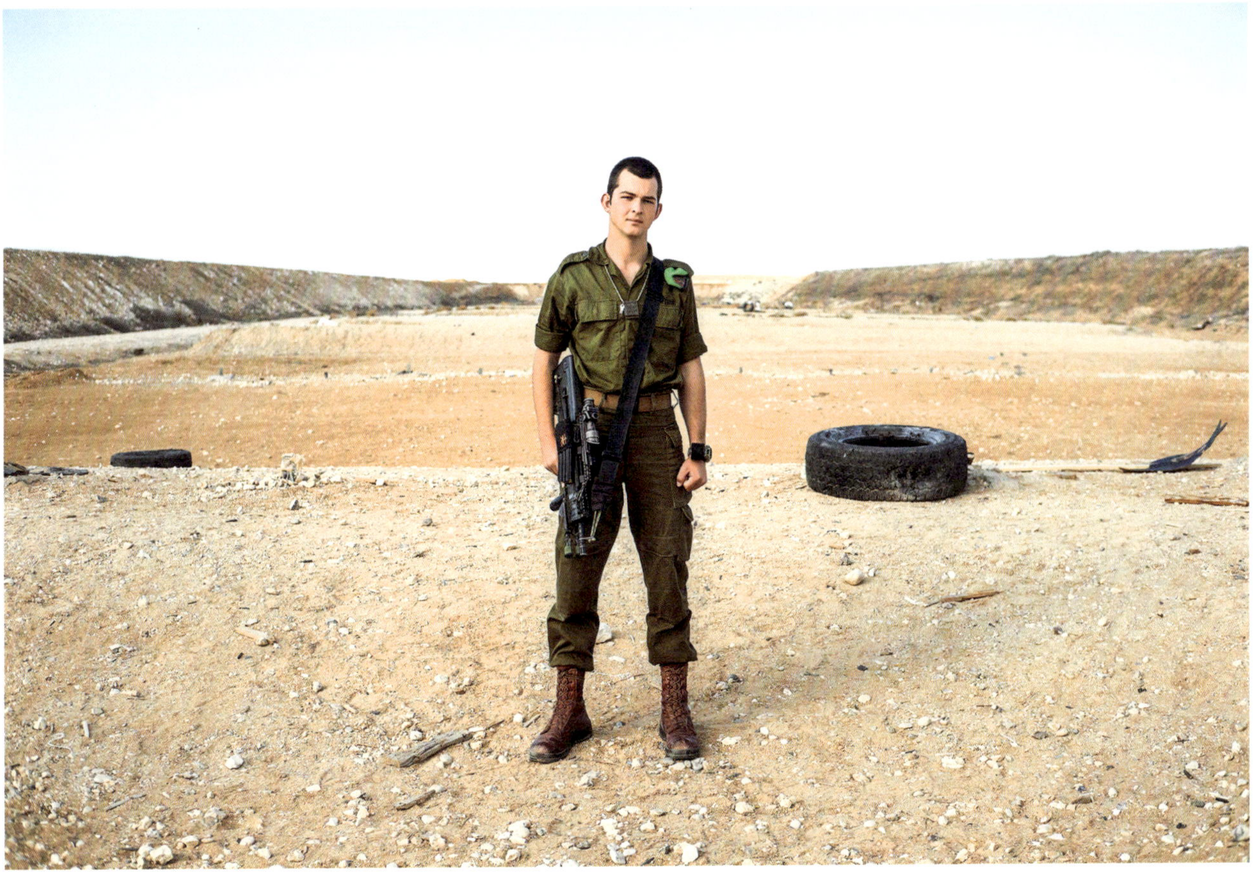

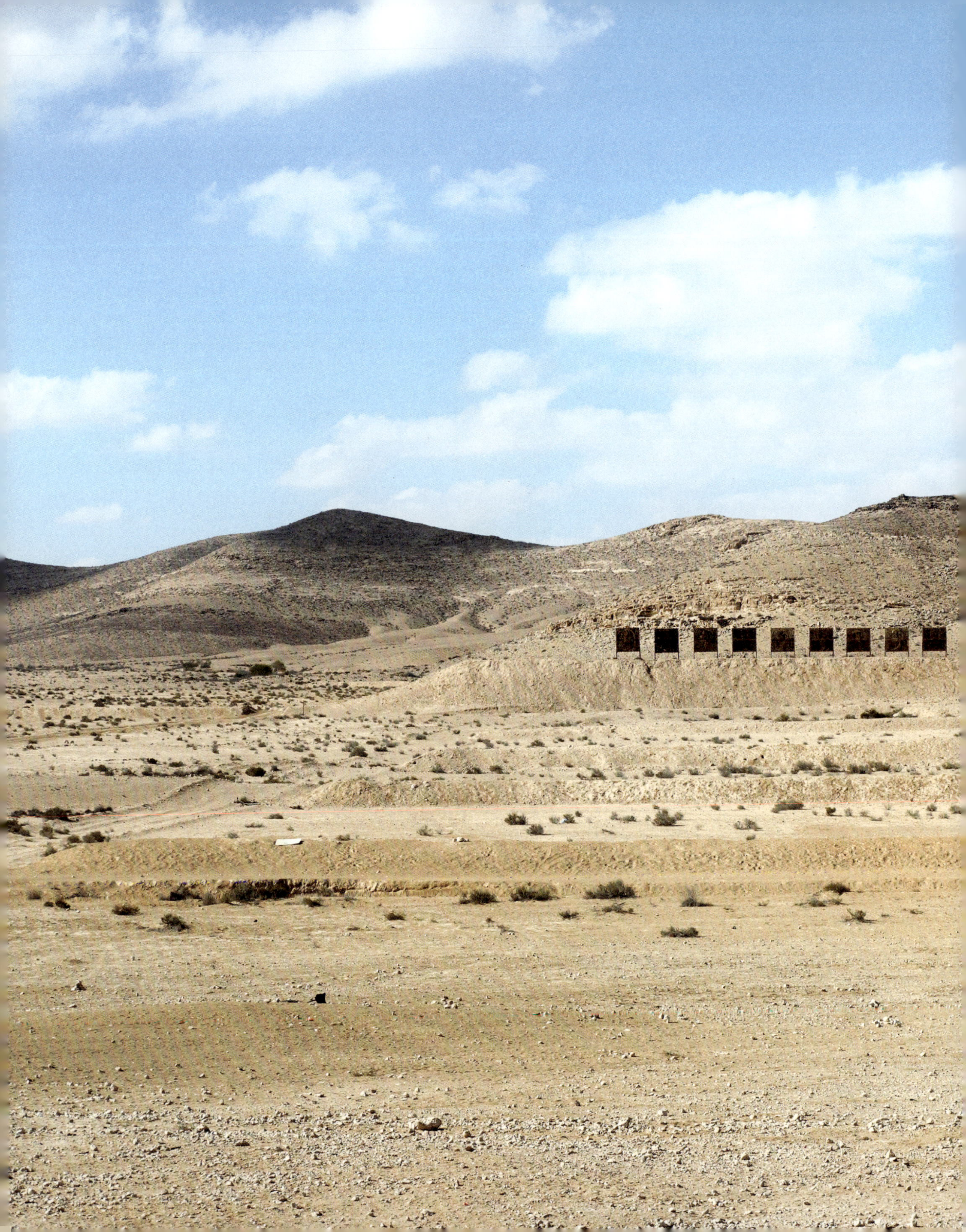

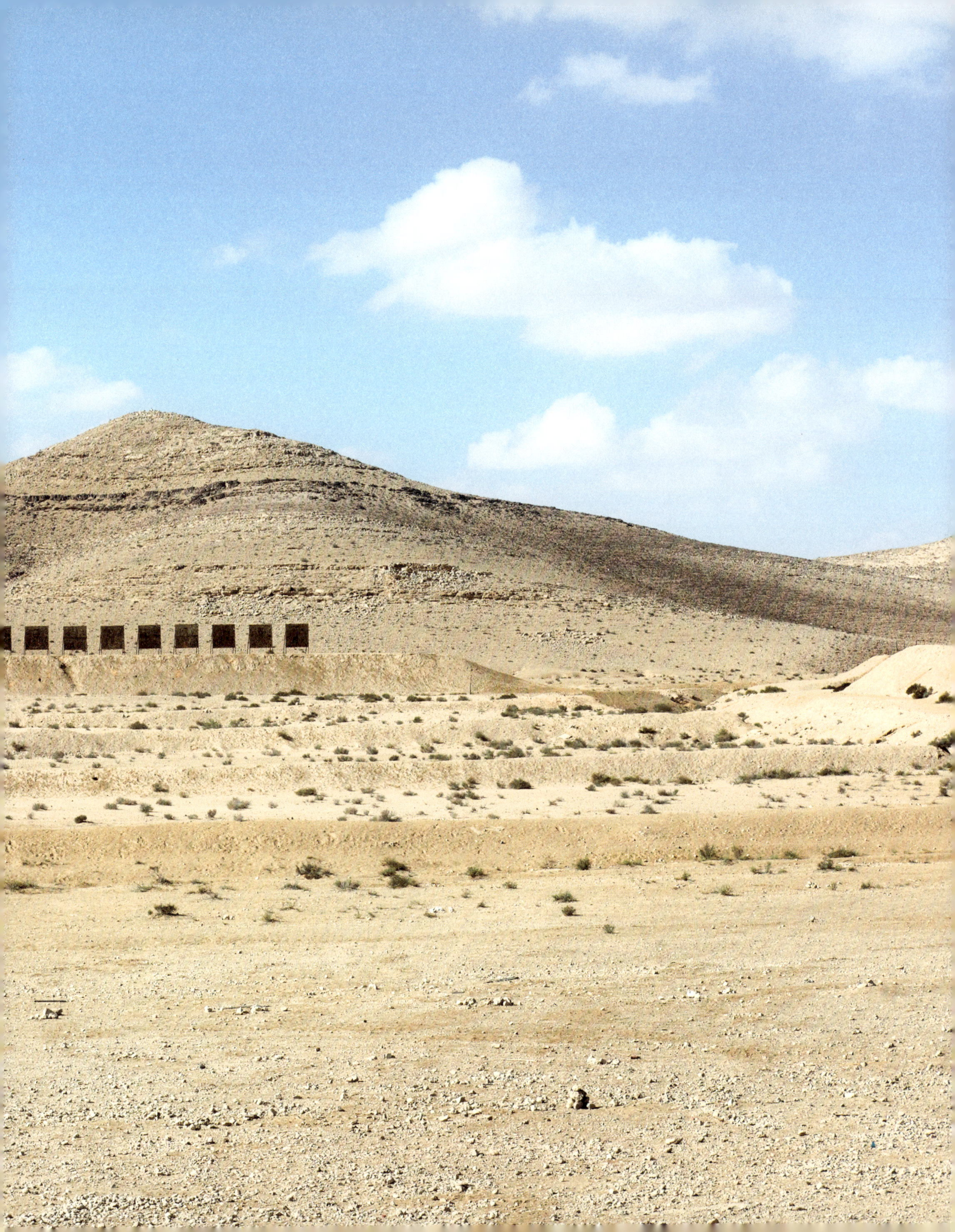

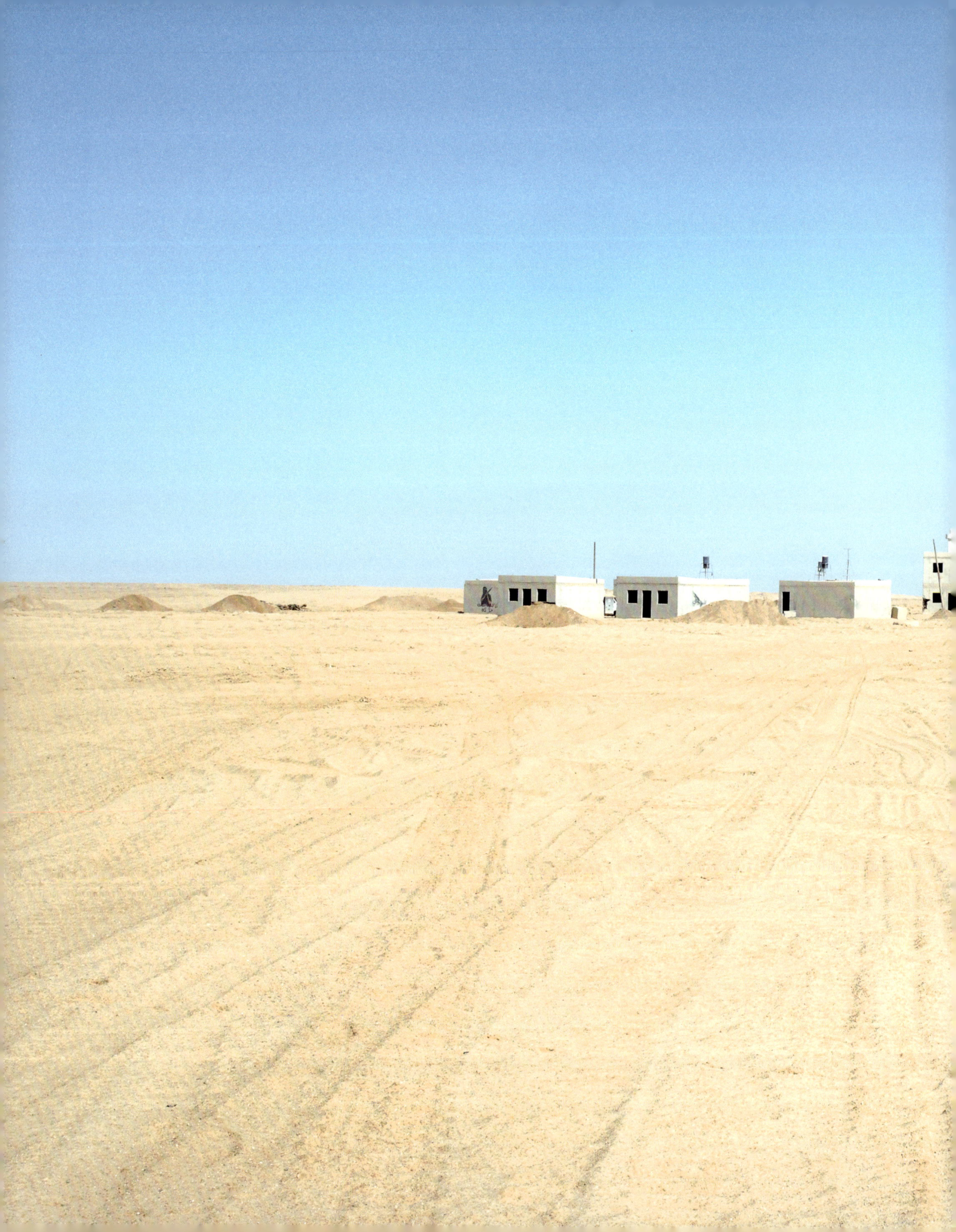

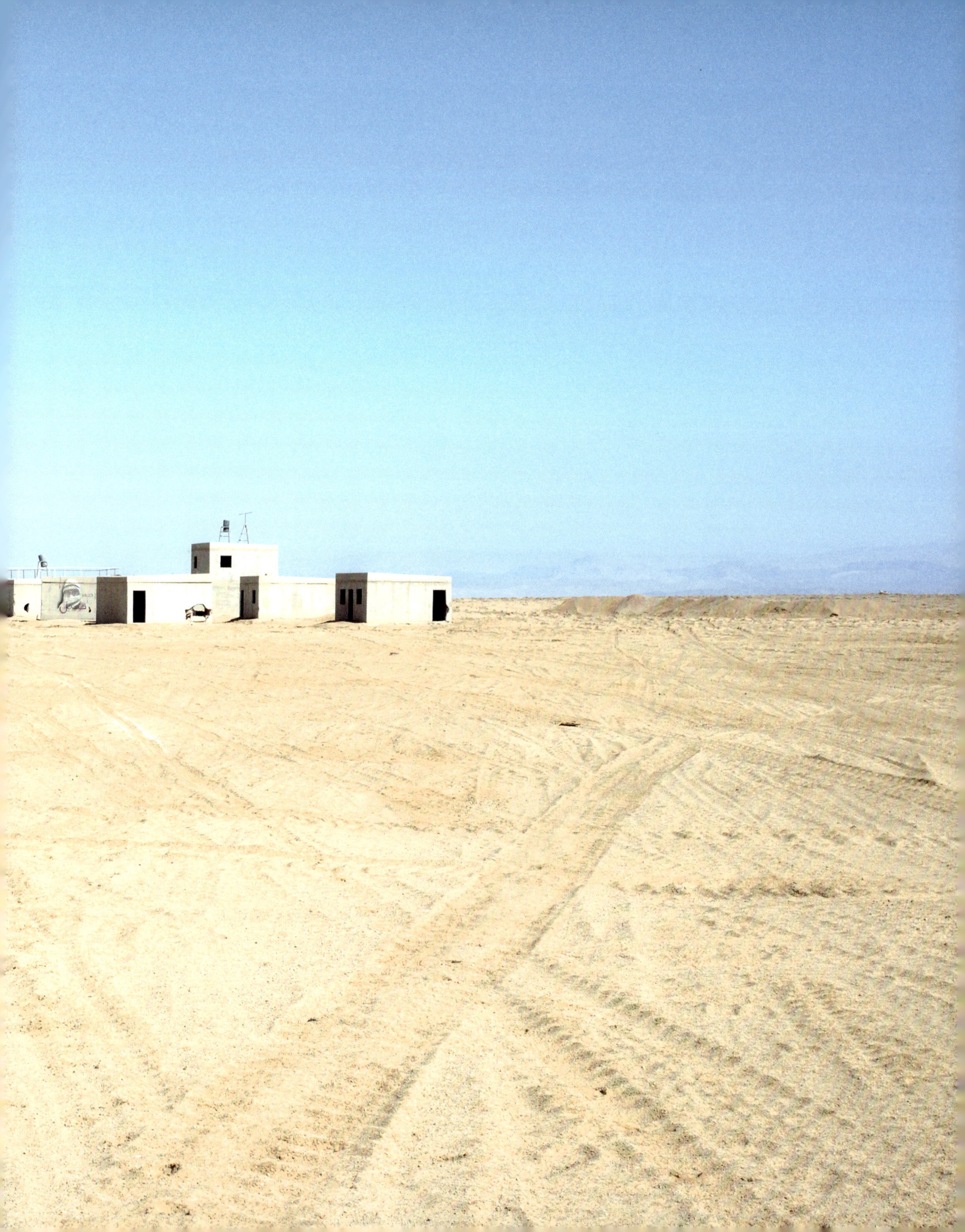

Belén | 19 | Córdoba, Argentina | Infantry

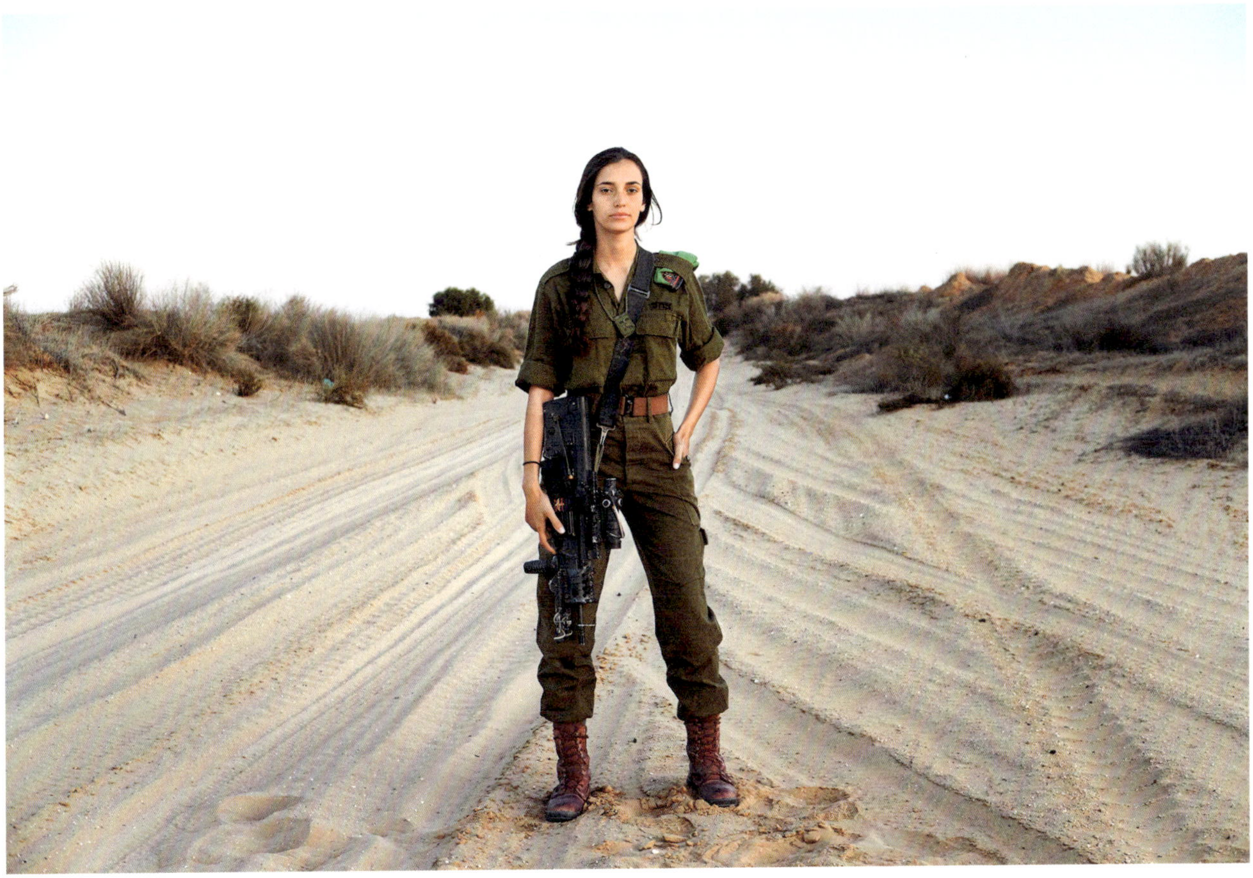

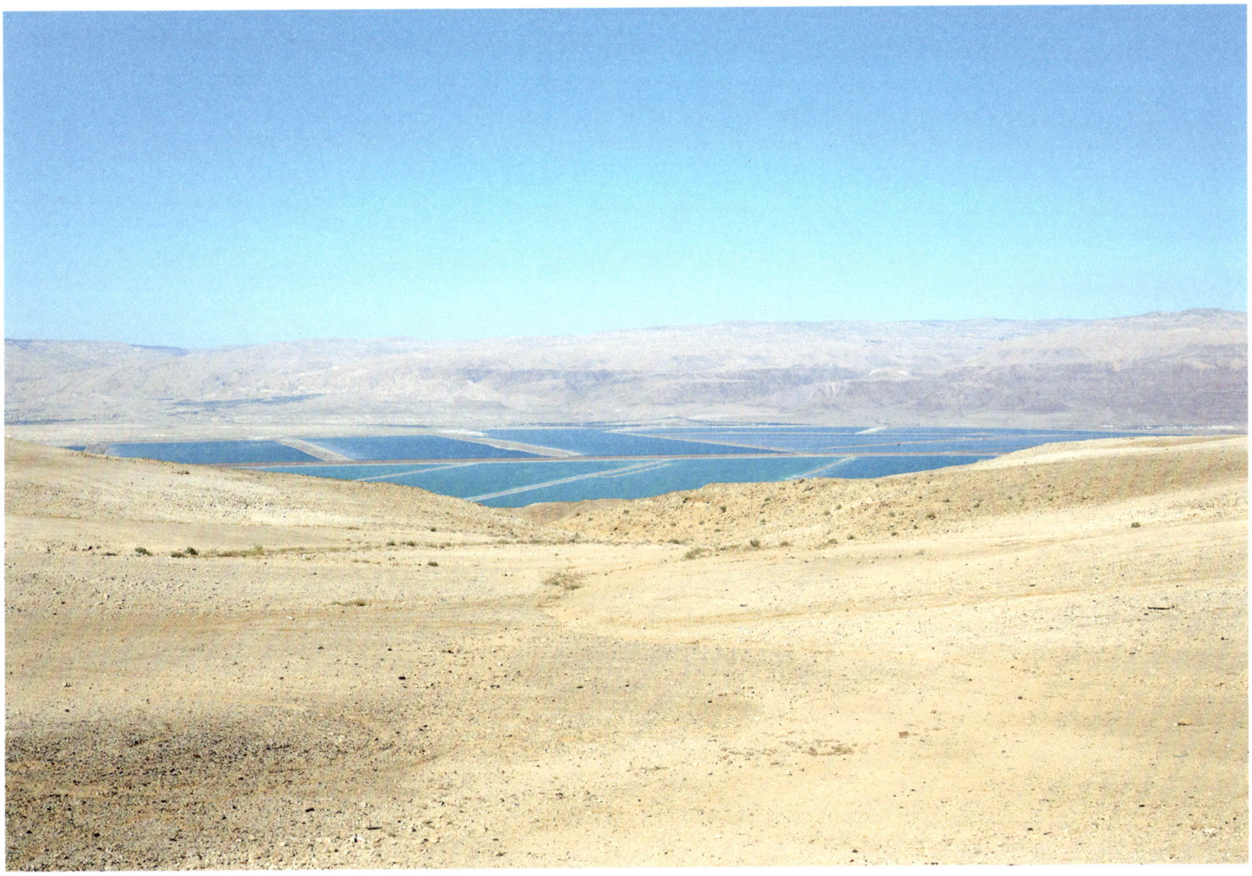

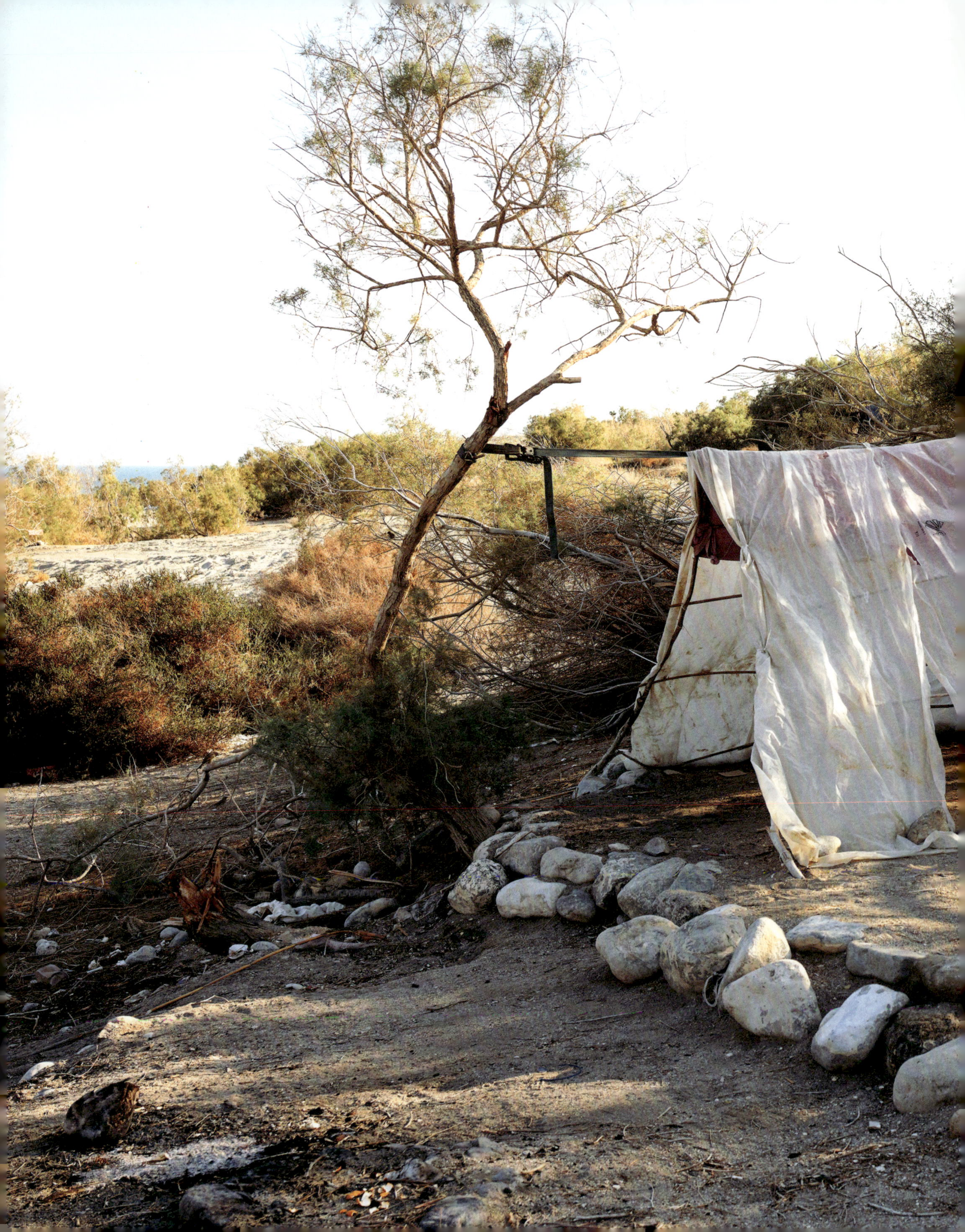

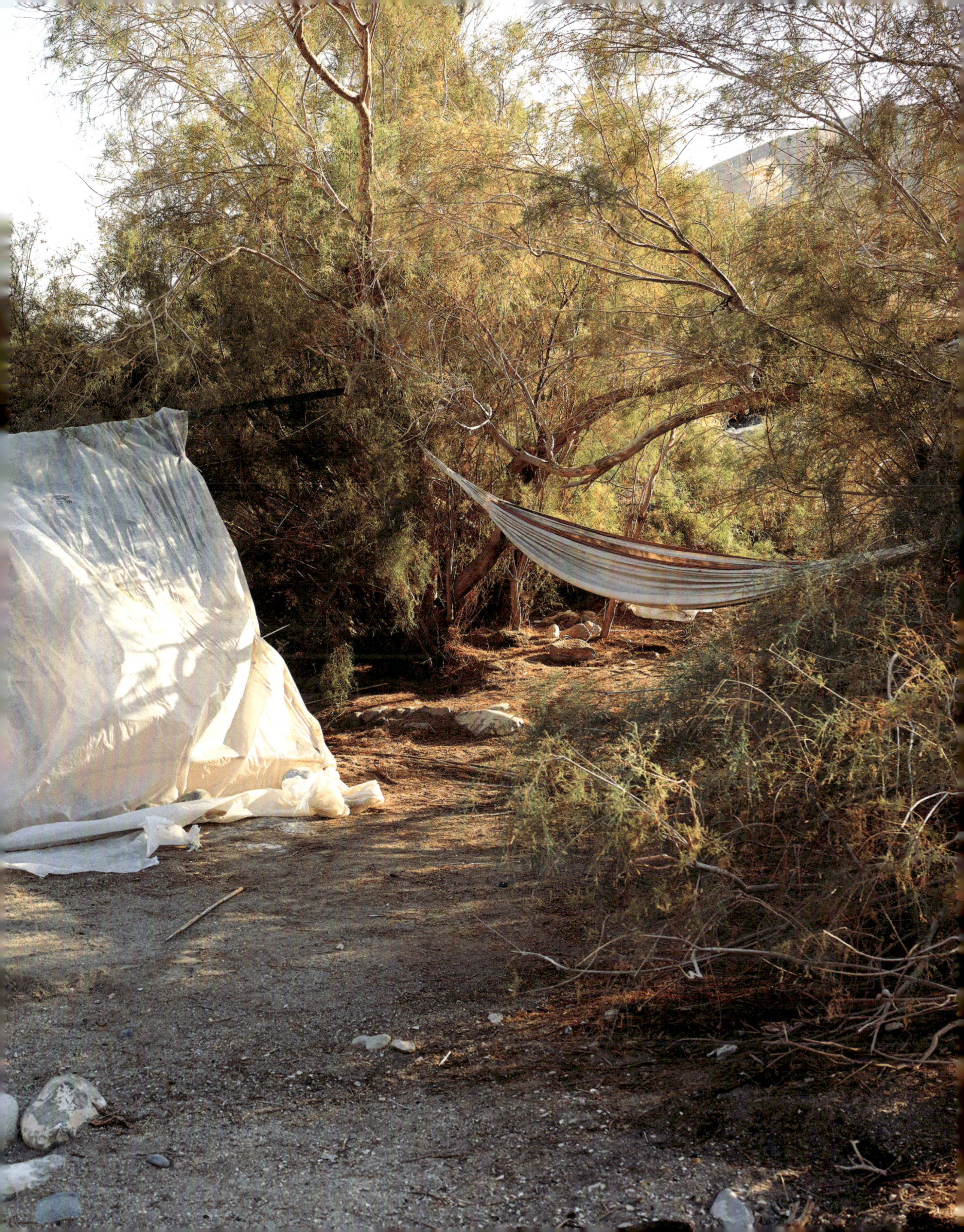

Gabrielle | 25 | Brisbane, Australia | Spokesperson's Unit

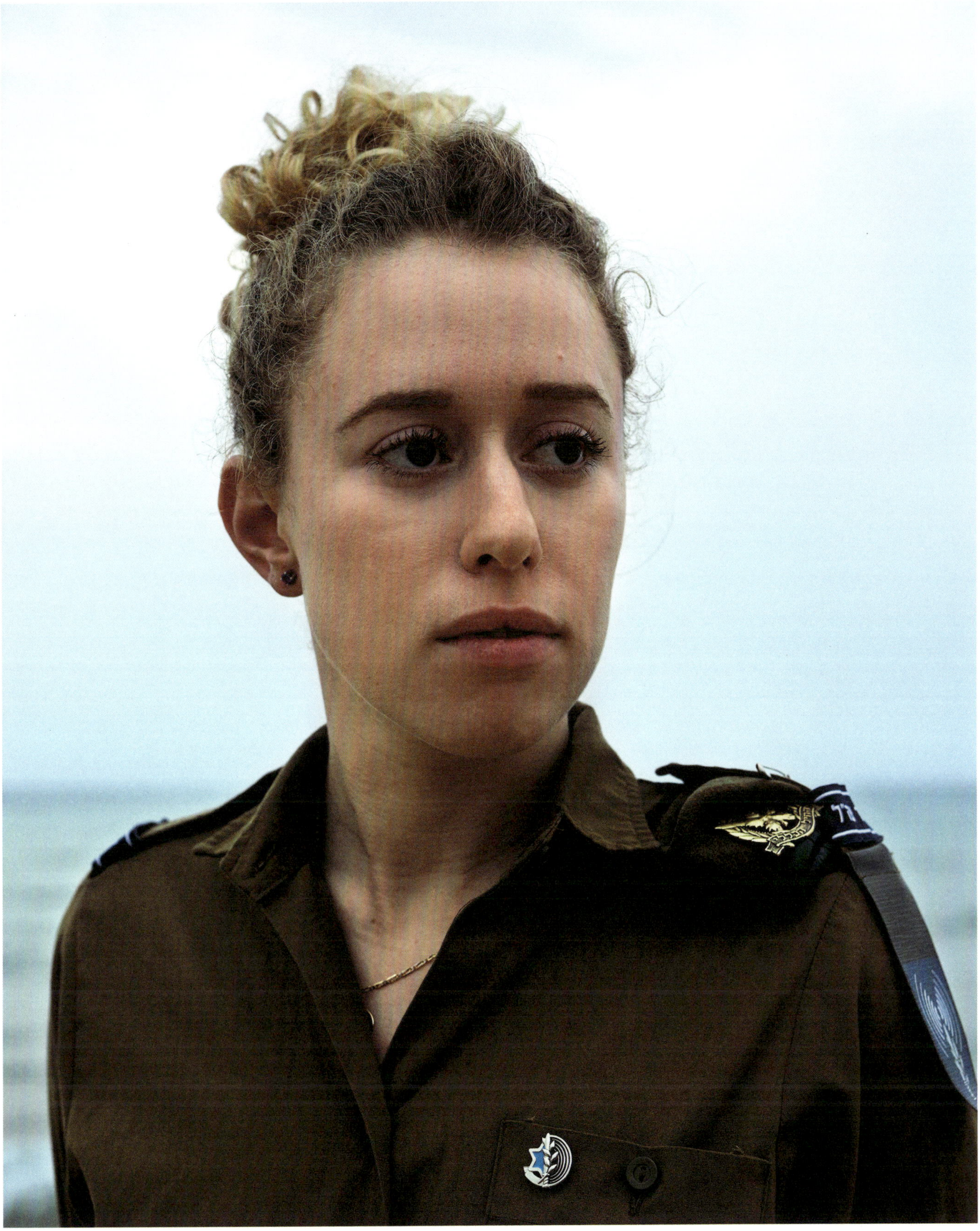

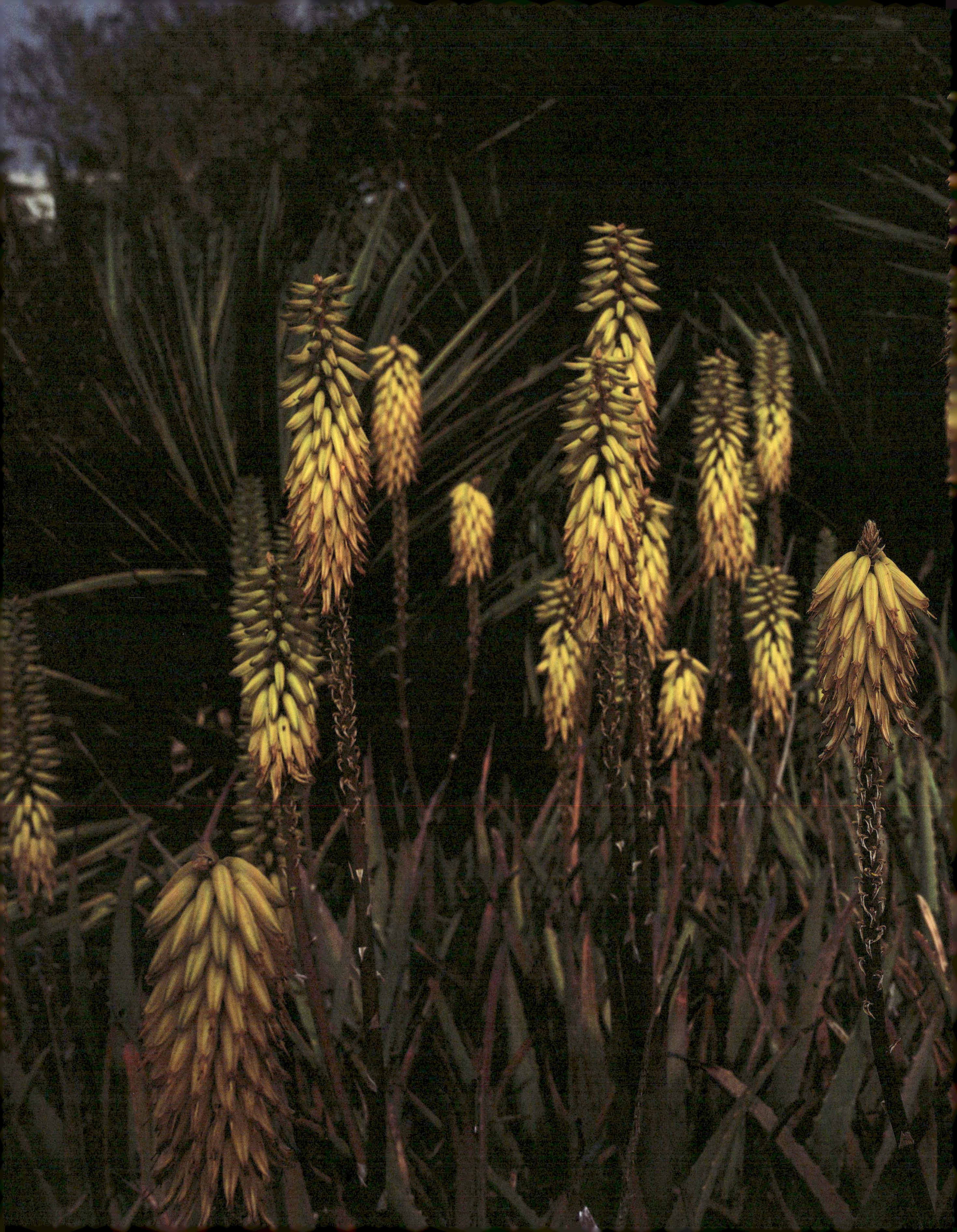

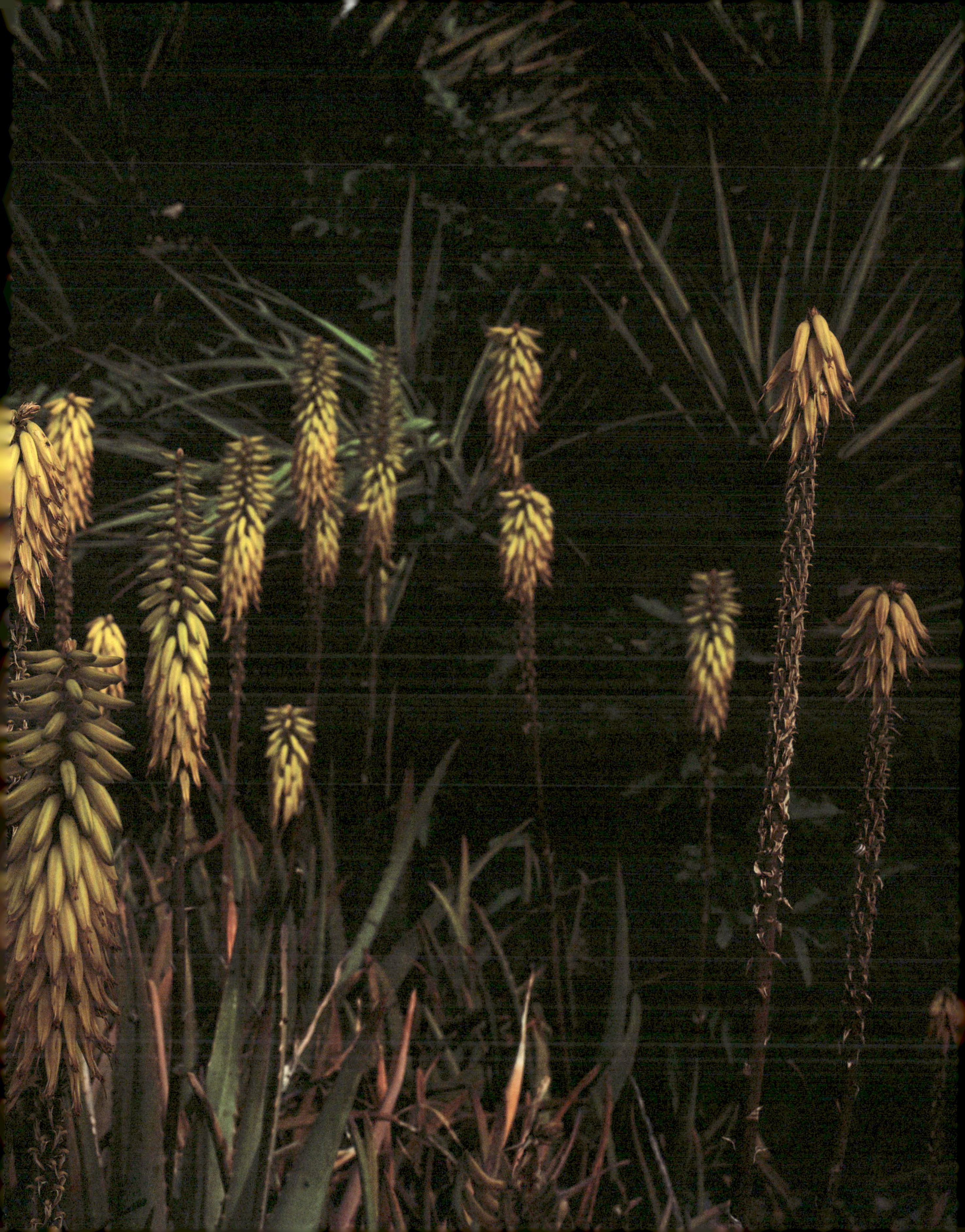

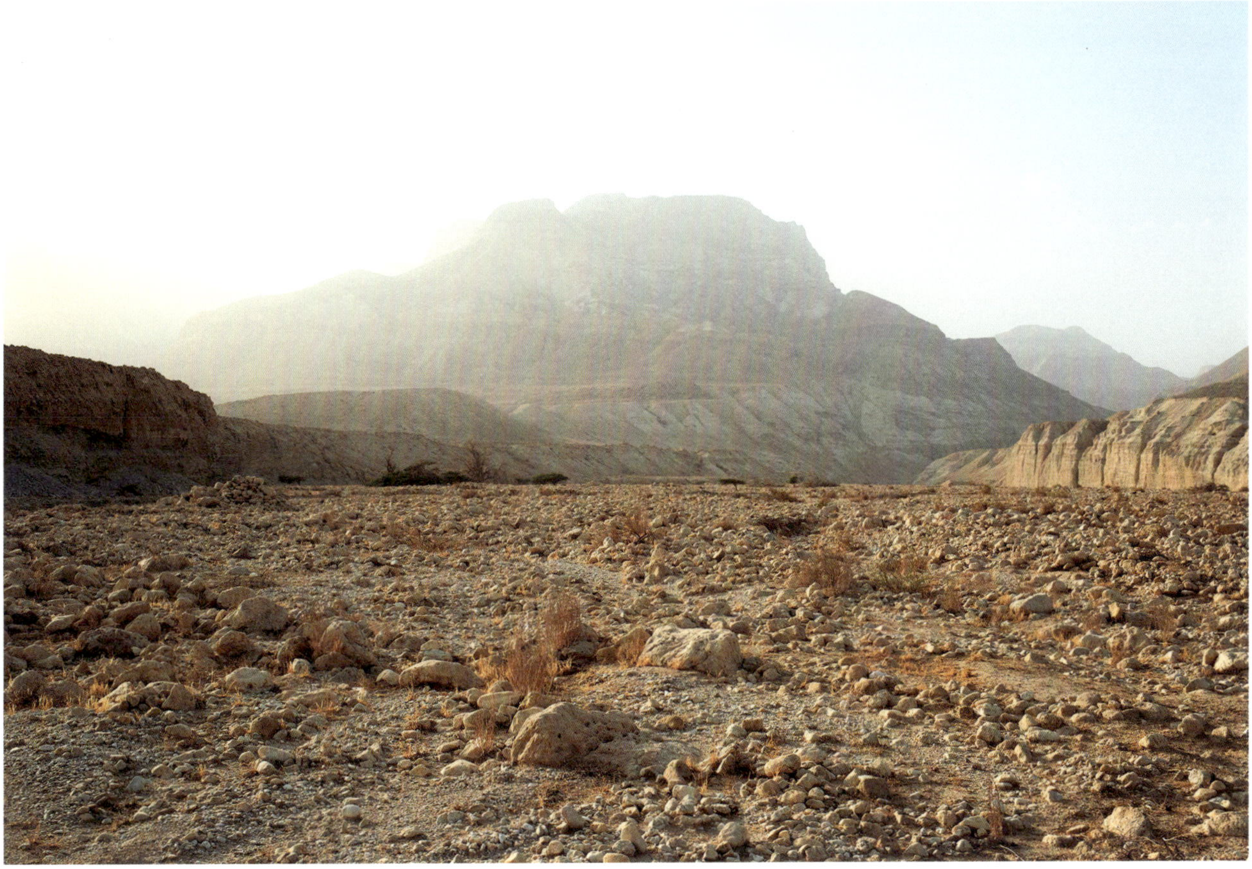

Bayli | 21 | Thornhill, Ontario, Canada | Infantry

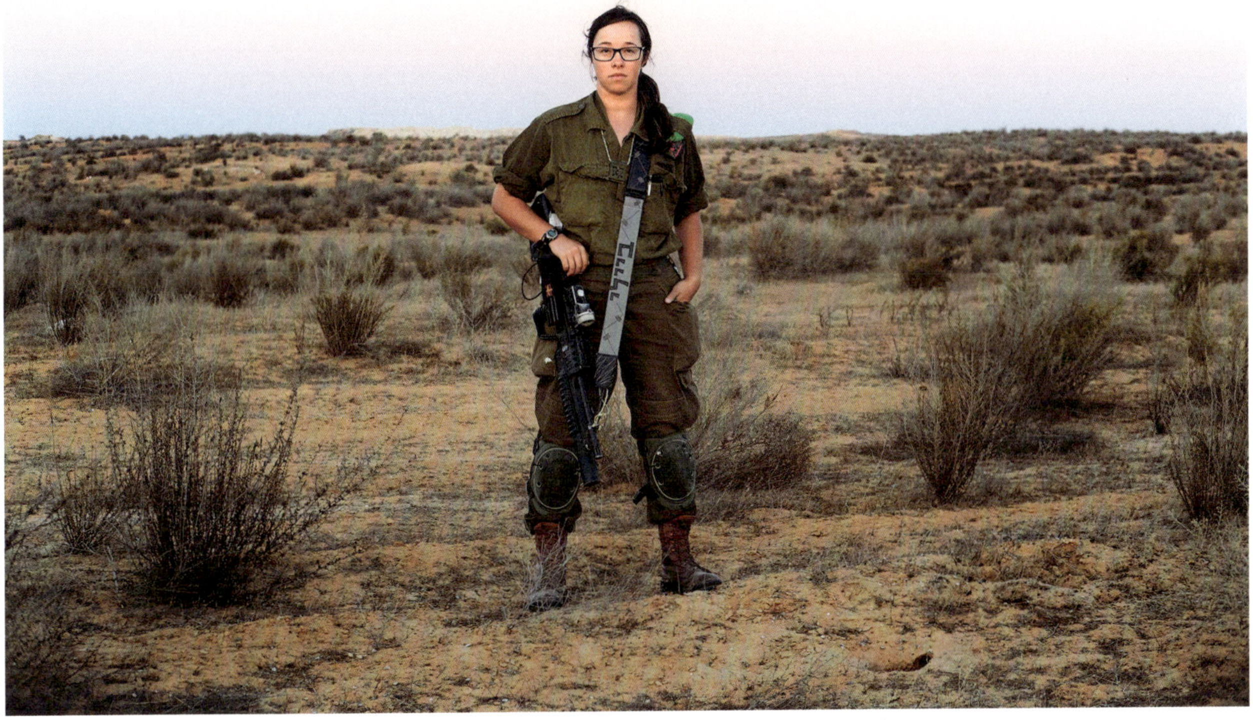

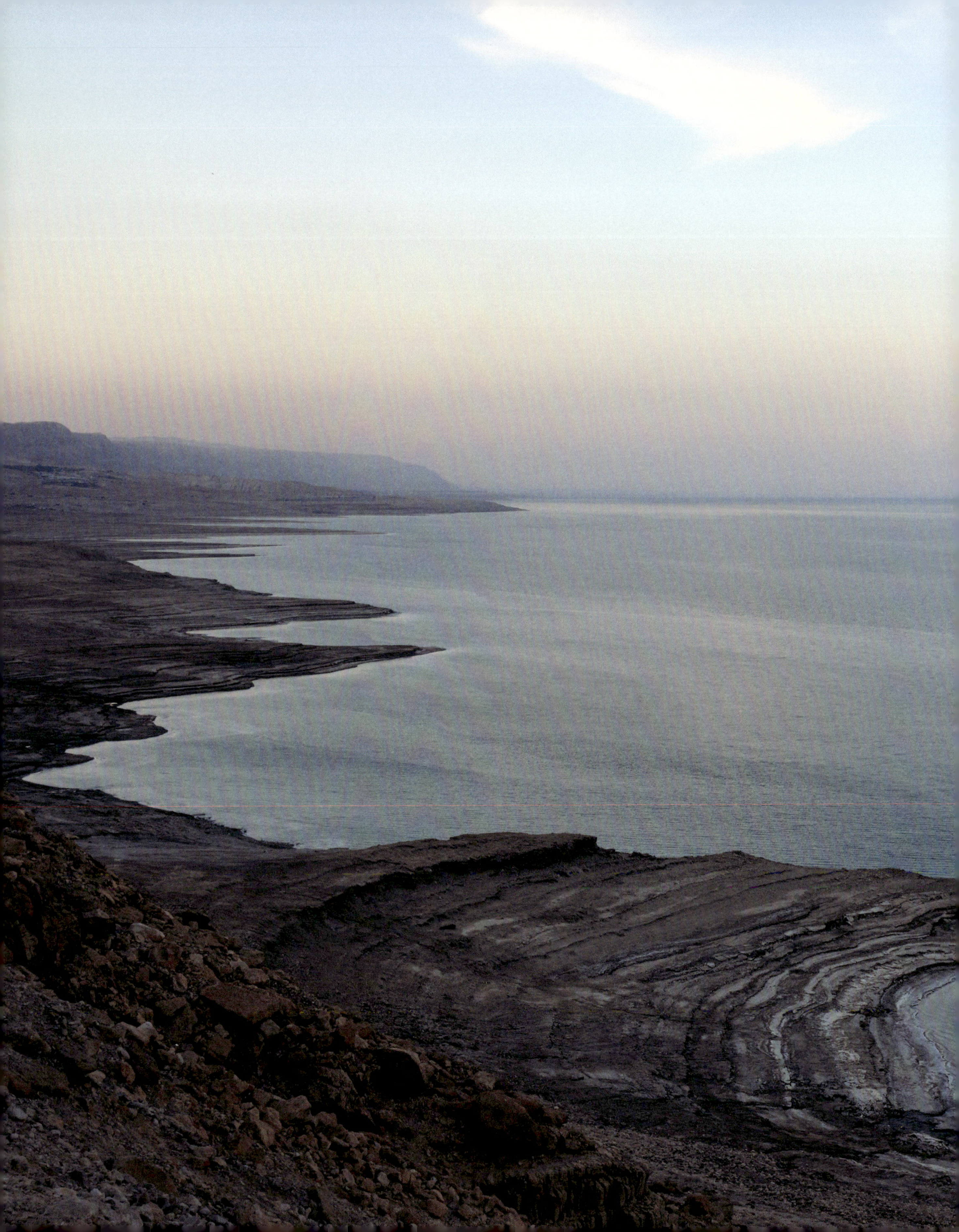

The Lone Soldiers of Israel and the Search for Belonging

When I joined an Israeli infantry unit in the summer of 1997, having moved from Toronto not long before, I discovered that army service in this country is the tail end of childhood. I was serving in an army of kids. The recruits I met that August, at a stark training base in the middle of the desert, had finished high school just a month before. Everyone – my new comrades, our sergeants and lieutenants – still lived in the same room they'd grown up in, with their teenage books and NBA posters and that 8th-grade jacket no one had bothered to throw out, and that's where they went back to on the weekends. I was just 19 myself. Envisioning a combat unit before I actually became part of one, I think I'd imagined something manlier – but our tent was full of care packages with homemade cookies. And there we were every evening, in fatigues a few sizes too big, lining up at the pay phones to call our mothers.

What allows you to get through army service, which is awful most of the time, is other people – your comrades, of course, but also your parents, who cook you a warm meal when you go home, do your laundry, and offer some sympathy and memories of their own time in uniform. Unlike soldiering in a country like America, which fights wars far away, here there are no overseas deployments and signing up doesn't mean leaving home. Unlike the Hollywood army movies about heroes fighting single-handedly, life in a real army, and certainly in this army, is plural. Getting a soldier through this time and safely out the other end is, for Israelis, a family project.

That explanation makes it easier to understand the unique Hebrew term at the heart of this photo project: chayalim bodedim, "lone soldiers." On the surface this is simply a technical designation used by the military, meaning a recruit is in Israel without parents and thus needs help in small ways – rent subsidies, for example, and more vacation time. But it's also a term indicating genuine disability, one to be pitied. In a communal and family-oriented society like Israel's, few things are worse than being "lone." My parents arrived in the country a few weeks before I was drafted, so I was lucky enough to be spared the designation. But we did have one "lone soldier" in our platoon, a kid from the former Soviet Union; he lasted a few months into basic training and then we never saw him again.

In one of my favourite images from Brant Slomovic's project, the armed soldier facing the camera is a 21-year-old from Addis Ababa. Like all the soldiers who appear in this book, Sisit is alone, accompanied only by the standard Israeli army trappings: a backdrop of desert hills, a rifle, a few rusted shipping containers. Her face is young but suggests she's crossed some ground to get here, that her own thoughts and decisions propelled her to this desolate base. Off-camera are her parents, siblings, friends back home. We grasp the existence of these other people out of our line of vision. Army service means the existence of comrades and enemies. But in the frame, in keeping with the photographer's design, there's no one but her.

When Brant interviewed his subjects about what led them into uniform, nearly none said anything about combat. There seemed to be little awareness of politics. What they talked about was belonging. A paratrooper named Daniel, for example, grew up almost 7,000 miles away in São Paulo, Brazil. But in his family of committed Zionists, he said, "I always heard about Israel, Israel, Israel," and he believed that "Israel is my home." When he visited at 16 and saw the soldiers on the streets and buses, teenagers just a few years older than he was, he decided that one day he'd be like them.

Another soldier, Samuel, sensed hostility in the country of his birth, Italy: "I felt that Milan wasn't my place," he told the photographer. "If I can't wear a kippah when I go around with my mom, if I don't feel secure, it makes me feel that it's not my home. I wasn't always comfortable, even in my neighbourhood, to reveal that I was Jewish. I was like a stranger in Italy even if I am Italian."

The irony in the stories of many of these "lone soldiers" is that many seem to have found their way here precisely because they were looking for an antidote to a feeling of estrangement, whether because of their Jewishness, or simply because of the broader isolation afflicting so many in Western societies. Yael, who grew up in Idaho and in California, was photographed while serving in a search-and-rescue unit along the Gaza border following the 2014 war with Hamas. She described hearing names of more and more soldiers, men her age, who'd been killed in the fighting. "Your heart just hurts," she said.

But she added:

> At the same time, I think that what I realized more is why I came here. To see the piles of [donated] clothes and food waiting for us at the gate of our base... Feeling that sense of community and so much support from complete strangers, ready to do anything for you, always voicing how much they support you, and how thankful they are that you are there. It was heart-wrenching to see all the names. Luckily, I didn't lose anybody. I feel like every time a soldier dies, it brings the country five steps closer. As horrible as that sounds, I think that's why we are still here. I try to explain it to my friends, but the sense that you have in Israel of family and belonging to complete strangers is unfathomable.

As the American journalist Sebastian Junger, who spent time with U.S. troops in Afghanistan and other war zones, wrote in "Tribe: On Homecoming and Belonging," studies show that humans need three key things in order to be happy. "They need to feel competent at what they do; they need to feel authentic in their lives; and they need to feel connected to others," he wrote. As communal ties and responsibilities become weaker in countries like the United States, the less happy people are, and the more prone to loneliness and depression. "Whatever the technological advances of modern society – and they're nearly miraculous – the individualized lifestyles that those technologies spawn seem to be deeply brutalizing to the human spirit," Junger observed. Despite its fractious politics, Israel remains a cohesive, even tribal, society when compared to countries in North America or Europe. And Israel's army is a tribe within a tribe.

Some of these soldiers are from Jewish homes where ideas about Israel played a central role. Others didn't know much about the place before they came. Some aren't Jewish according to strict rabbinic law, according to which Judaism is passed down only by the mother. One soldier said she wasn't sure if her mother was Jewish or not. The features of the soldiers – from Thailand, Canada, Kazakhstan, Argentina, Peru, Ethiopia – are the features of the entire planet. But the same thread runs through all of the stories of the lone soldiers who appear here: They've come a long way to join their fate to the fate of others.

Matti Friedman, an Israeli journalist, is the author of "Pumpkinflowers: A Soldier's Story of a Forgotten War." He served in an Israeli infantry unit from 1997–2000, and in the reserves until 2016. Matti's other nonfiction books are "The Aleppo Codex" and "Spies of No Country." He was born in Toronto and lives in Jerusalem.

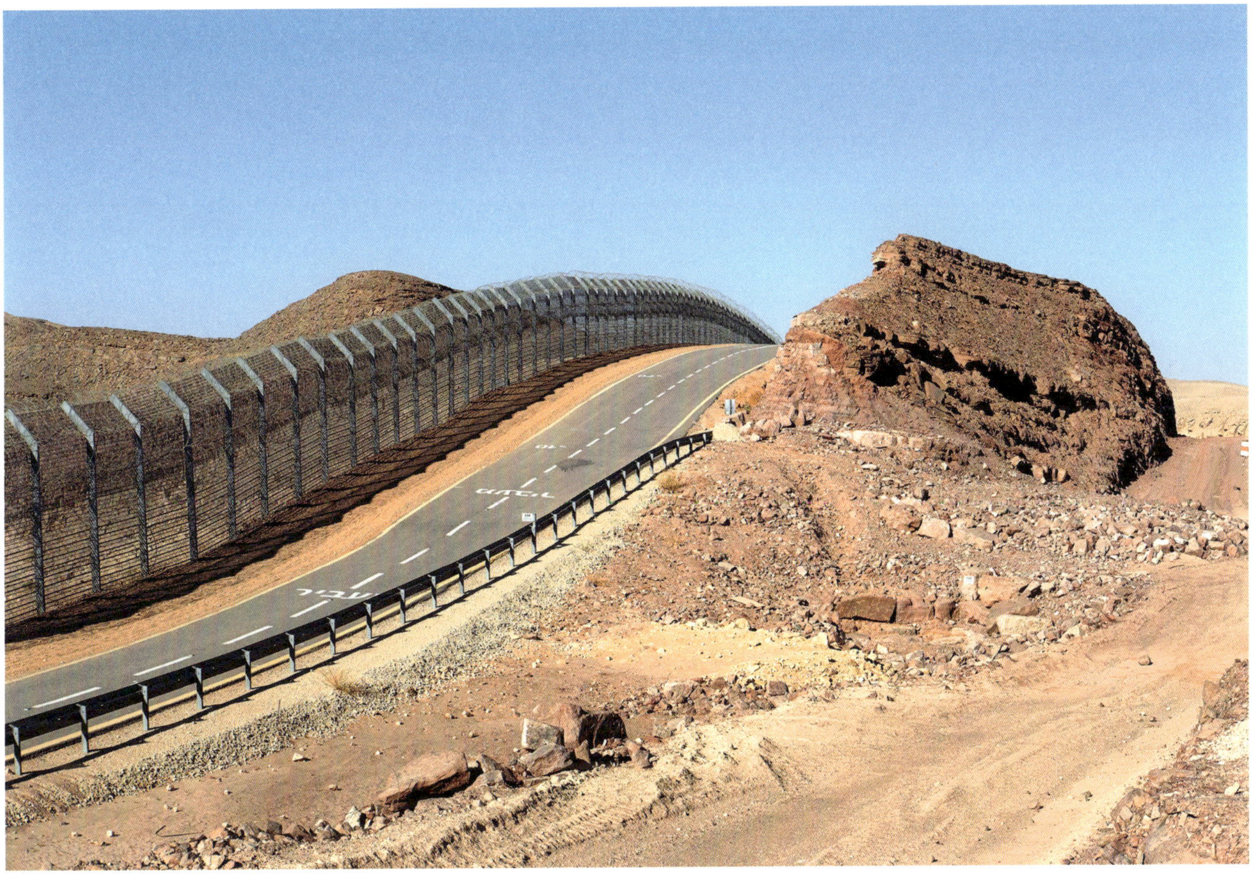

Acknowledgements

For Yasmin – absent your love, and unwavering support and encouragement, none of this would be possible. I love you.

To Mom and Dad – thank you, I love you.

My heartfelt gratitude to all the lone soldiers who placed trust in me and were so generous in sharing their stories.

Thank you Jan Rosseel for your friendship and collaboration, and for the fantastic design.

Matti Friedman, I'm immensely grateful for your contribution and your meaningful words that accompany the images.

Thank you Alexa Becker, and the team at Kehrer Verlag (Klaus Kehrer, Julia Frohnhoff, René Henoch, Barbara Karpf) who believed in this work from the beginning, and welcomed me into the family.

Thank you to my dear friends and colleagues in Canada, Israel, and abroad, who have shared their time and talents, guidance and inspiration:

Dany Cushmaro, Sivan Abergil, Yaakov & Maya Israel, Ilia Yefimovich, Guy Shamai, The Israeli Defense Force Spokesperson's Unit, Dalia Schlesinger & Shimon Yaffe, Judy Maltz, Faiz Abu Rmeleh, Noi Einav, Clement Chapillon, Naomi Harris, Daniel Seguin, Donald Weber, Simon Roberts, Kalpesh Lathigra, Stephen Brookbank, Charlotte Cotton, Clare Vander Meersch, Stephen Bulger, Gaëlle Morel, Cheryl Newman, Alison Nordstrom, Teun van der Heijden, Fiona Shields, Emma Bowkett, Alessia Glaviano, Genevieve Fussell, Laura Pressley, Shane Lavalette, Clinton Cargill, Howard Tanenbaum, Adam Gomolin, George Emerson, Lewis Tepper, Steve Herskovitz, Gary Lebovics, Aryeh Elbaz, Mark Shekter, Yoni Freedhoff, and the team at Toronto Image Works (Jeannie Baxter, Francine Lemieux, Dan Ebert, Jill McCrie, Eric Zeiburlins).

Concept / Brant Slomovic and Jan Rosseel
Text / Matti Friedman
Project Management / Kehrer Verlag (Julia Frohnhoff)
Copy Editing / Alex Mlynek
Image Processing / Dan Ebert and Kehrer Design (René Henoch)
Design / Jan Rosseel
Production Management / Kehrer Design (Tom Streicher)
Cover Illustration / Jan Rosseel

Bibliographic information published by the Deutsche Nationalbibliothek
The Deutsche Nationalbibliothek lists this publication in the Deutsche Nationalbibliografie; detailed bibliographic data is available on the Internet at http://dnb.dnb.de.

Printed and bound in Germany
ISBN 978-3-86828-980-0

Kehrer Heidelberg Berlin
www.kehrerverlag.com